Wildlife of the North

Wildlife of the North

Animals of the High Latitudes of North America and Europe

Hälle Flygare • Valerius Geist • Geoffrey Holroyd • Wayne Lynch

FIREFLY BOOKS

A FIREFLY BOOK

Published by Firefly Books Ltd. 2023

First printing

Library of Congress Control Number: 2023936364

Library and Archives Canada Cataloguing in Publication
Title: Wildlife of the North : animals of the high latitudes of North America and Europe /
     Hälle Flygare, Valerius Geist, Geoffrey Holroyd, Wayne Lynch.
Names: Flygare, Hälle, 1936- author, photographer. | Geist, Valerius, author. |
     Holroyd, Geoffrey L., author. | Lynch, Wayne, author.
Description: Includes bibliographical references and index.
Identifiers: Canadiana 2023022038X | ISBN 9780228104551 (softcover)
Subjects: LCSH: Animals—Arctic regions—Pictorial works. |
     LCSH: Wildlife photography—Arctic regions. | LCSH: Animals—Arctic regions. |
     LCSH: Climatic changes—Arctic regions. | LCGFT: Illustrated works.
Classification: LCC QL105 .F59 2023 | DDC 591.70911/3—dc23

Published in the United States by
Firefly Books (U.S.) Inc.
P.O. Box 1338, Ellicott Station
Buffalo, New York 14205

Published in Canada by
Firefly Books Ltd.
50 Staples Avenue, Unit 1
Richmond Hill, Ontario L4B 0A7

Cover and interior design: Hälle Flygare
Digital layout: Linda Petras
Artwork: Valerius Geist
Scientific edit: Stephen Stringham
Editors: Rob Alexander, Ann-Charlotte Berglund and Linda Flygare
Arctic map: Wikimedia

Printed in China

Map of the Arctic, with the Arctic Circle (blue) and July + 10°C isotherm temperature (red), closely corresponding to the treeline and defining the boundary between tundra and taiga. (Wikimedia).

CONTENTS

The Story Behind This Book

Hälle Flygare

My interest in photography began at a very young age, when I worked at a local camera store for three seasons in my Swedish hometown of Hörby developing film and printing black-and-white pictures. I purchased my Exakta 35mm camera, together with a long telephoto lens, as I was interested in bird photography.

In my youth I read fascinating tales of Swedish-Canadian trappers. Their courage and experiences in the wilds of Canada fed my dreams to emigrate and live in the Canadian wilderness.

I also met Åke Sjöström, a forestry student who encouraged me to pursue a forestry career, which took me from southern Sweden to northern Lappland. Swedish military service was followed by emigration to Canada where I continued working in forestry and also obtained a big game hunting licence.

In 1973, I became a Park Warden in Banff National Park. While guiding moose hunters in Tweedsmuir Provincial Park in British Columbia I came across long forgotten Native trails, which were used by Alexander Mackenzie searching for a trade route across Canada to the Pacific Ocean. He accomplished this July 22, 1793, making him the first white man to successfully cross the North American continent. Through my efforts to protect this historic trail I was seconded in 1975 by Parks Canada in Ottawa to do an inventory of the Alexander Mackenzie Historic Trail. It is a 347 km ancient trade route used by Nuxalk and Carrier First Nations that runs from the Fraser River to Bella Coola on the Pacific Coast. I received the Annual Award of Honour from the Heritage Society of British Columbia in 1989 for my contribution to the project.

After leaving the Park Service, I devoted all my time to the camera, traveling and guiding wildlife photo tours. My photographs have been published in leading nature magazines throughout the world and I have authored several books published in Sweden, *Storvilt i Canada* and *Buffelmarker* and in Canada, *In The Steps of Alexander Mackenzie* and *Sir Alexander Mackenzie Waterways in Alberta*. My wildflower images illustrate two best selling flower books, *Wildflowers of the Canadian Rockies* and *Wildflowers of the Rocky Mountains*. Since 1962 wildlife and nature photography has encouraged me to travel in Africa, Asia, Antarctica, Alaska, Canada, Sweden, Finland and Norway's Svalbard.

For this book, I needed additional pictures to showcase the greatest wilderness on earth. Searching for the very best arctic images from professional photographers worldwide was a big task that took several years.

I am grateful to Dr. Valerius Geist, Dr. Geoffrey Holroyd and Dr. Wayne Lynch, three outstanding scientists in their fields for writing the text, including Dr. Geist's line drawings of ice age mammals. Without their contributions this book would not have materialized. I am also indebted to Dr. Stephen Stringham and Ann-Charlotte Berglund for their editing. I have received generous permission from Robert Berdan, Rinie Van Meurs, Ewald Popp, Stefan Johansson, Peter Ericksson, Philippe Henry, Sture Traneving and Peter Perren to reproduce their excellent images. Above all, I thank my wife Linda for sharing my life and dreams as a writer and wildlife photographer and for traveling with me in the wilderness under sometimes difficult circumstances.

Hälle Flygare relaxing on the arctic tundra east of Great Bear Lake, Northwest Territories, Canada. Robert Berdan Photo.
www.natureinwildplaces.com

Foreword

Stephen Stringham

This book struck me with its superb photography — sharp, well composed, colorful, and informative. The text is a delightful surprise. All too often in illustrated books, stunning images are accompanied by trivial text that merely rephrases second hand information, or worse. Thanks to the expertise and diversity of its authors, this book is equally rich in images and fresh facts.

This book is celebration of arctic and subarctic wildlife but also a reminder of the great peril awaiting us, if climate change and human impacts continue. Some species may face extinction in the foreseeable future.

So it was with joyful anticipation that I opened the book to find that the beginning chapters of Ice Age Survivors was written by Valerius Geist. He is one of the world's foremost paleo-ethologists, an expert on the evolution, extinction, biogeography, ecology and behavior of northern hemisphere ungulates — i.e. hoofstock. His six chapters provide information about a diversity of ungulates, carnivores, rodents, and lagomorphs and are enriched with Geist's insights on the habitat and other creatures together with which the species evolved.

Equally impressive are Geoffrey Holroyd's chapters presenting a stunning photographic panorama of arctic birds. The text is rich in intriguing contrasts and comparisons of ecology and behavior among species. Readers are also treated to Hälle Flygare's chapter on arctic plants and some of the more colorful and welcome insects, not including those that buzz and bite, suck or sting.

The text concludes with Wayne Lynch's chapter on the arctic habitat itself, and how it is rapidly changing under the onslaught of climate warming — faster than many species can adapt to. Lynch reminds us that during periods of abrupt habitat transformation, even the most beautiful and tenacious life forms are fragile. His glimpse of a potentially tragic future also shows the parallel comparison of how the Northern Hemisphere and its biota were transformed at the end of the last Ice Age. This is both chilling and enlightening.

By enhancing our appreciation for surviving arctic wildlife and wildlands, these authors gently remind us of how much more our lives might have been enriched, had not so many fantastic and fascinating creatures not already been driven to extinction. Just as we will never have an opportunity to know those bygone creatures, our own descendants may never know the spectacular animals which we still take for granted. The longer we hesitate to implement long term conservation strategies, the more species and ecosystems will be lost.

While guiding students and wildlife viewers, I have carried all sorts of field manuals to educate about the animals we can see at any place and time, and how they relate to the many other species that we can't see. None of the manuals I found are as attractive and useful for this purpose.

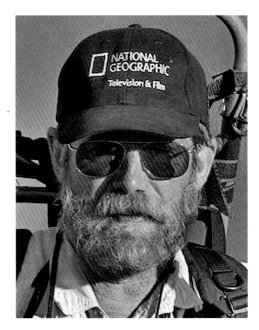

Stephen F. Stringham, PhD
Director, Bear Communication & Coexistence Research Program.
www.bear-viewing-in-alaska.info

Mountain goat (*Oreamnos americanus*). A billy goat high above timberline. Jasper National Park, Canada.

CHAPTER ONE

Ice Age Survivors

Mountain Goat

The mountain goat is an enigma, strikingly different from any other cloven-hoofed animal. Obviously, it is adapted to environmental extremes. Just watch a male on a sunny February day high above timberline, striding calmly up a ridge while gale-force winds tear at his longhaired white coat. We do not know when and how this animal came to America. Mountains are poor places to find fossils and we know of past goats only from remains in caves. One cave deep in the Grand Canyon has remains dating back 40,000 years to the middle of the last glaciation. There is no trace of a relative in Siberia where it had to come from. A few fragmented fossil bones have been found as far south as Arizona where the goats were dwarfs. That and the enlarged teeth indicate a diet of chronically poor quality vegetation.

Life for mountain goats revolves around the adult female with her young. When winter conditions are difficult, the female claims a territory on a steep sun-exposed cliff just for herself and her young and kicks away all other goats. Big adult breeding males leave readily. Adolescent males which have not mated are reluctant, but the female usually prevails. Goat horns are weapons of devilishly clever design. A quick stab can end in death and the horns have to be quickly withdrawn before the victim's thrashing can end in death and the horns break from the goat's rather fragile skull. Mountain goats have killed dogs, wolves, grizzly bears and people. Although billies carry dermal skull armor almost an inch thick, during rutting battles they still injure each other severely with multiple puncture wounds and tears. So they fight rarely, relying heavily on bluff charges. Although females sometimes use their horns against billies, males rarely retaliate, much less attack females.

Nanny goat with newborn kid on a sun-exposed cliff in the front range of the Rocky Mountains. Mt. Evans, Colorado, USA.

Dall's sheep (*Ovis dalli*). This sheep inhabits Alaska's Chugach and Wrangle Mountains. Other sheep species inhabit the Pacific Coast Range down to Oregon and the Rocky Mountains as far south as Colorado. Across the Bering Strait in northeast Siberia, the Dall's closest relative is the snow sheep (*Ovis nivicola*). Denali National Park, Alaska, USA.

Dall's and Bighorn Sheep

Siberia is home to snow sheep (*Ovis nivicola*). During or after the last ice age, some migrated to North America, giving rise to the thin-horned Dall's sheep (*Ovis dalli*) — named in honor of the early explorer-biologist William Healey Dall. They now exist mainly in Alaska and northern Canada. The pure white Dall's sheep is striking when juxtaposed with its neighbor in British Columbia's coastal mountains, the dark, often black, Stone's sheep (named after the American explorer A. J. Stone). The next species to the south is the American bighorn sheep (*Ovis canadensis*).

There are striking differences among bighorns from different habitats. For instance, compare desert bighorns from

Bighorn sheep (*Ovis canadensis*). Bighorn sheep are fairly common in the Rocky Mountains, from southern Canada to New Mexico. From near extinction with a few thousand left in the early 1900s, the population today has recovered to about 50,000 to 70,000 sheep. Jasper National Park, Canada.

the American southwest and Mexico to the cold-adapted northern Rocky Mountain bighorns. The huge horns of the old males are exceptionally thick and heavy, up to 14 kg. They are weapons, wielded like a karate chop, focusing the energy of the blow on the keel of the horn. The opponent catches the blows with his own horns and skull. These are in effect armor, forming a helmet-like double layer of tough, thick, spongy, shock-absorbing bone over the brain. Right after a clash the rivals show their horns allowing each other to compare the severity of the blow. The bigger the horns, the harder the blow, and the higher the social rank of the bearer. The loser does not leave the herd but stays and submits to being courted and mounted like a female by the winner. Large horns are grown by

animals with access to either superior food or in secure terrain. Large-horned rams are of intense interest to young males, which have not yet acquired a string of seasonal home ranges of their own. By following the largest horned rams, youngsters learn about the best feeding sites and the most secure escape terrain. However, that is not in the interest of the biggest-horned rams as the young fellows, of course, will eat them out of house and home! The smaller rams overcome the elder's resistance by exactly mimicking the behavior of a female in heat ready to be bred. That flirting is irresistible to the big rams. Mountain sheep maintain their distribution via a tradition of exploiting a series of small, often tiny, far-flung areas of habitat, a tradition passed on from the old to the young, generation after generation.

Barren-ground caribou (*Rangifer tarandus groenlandicus*). The caribou is a migrating species. The Porcupine Herd makes the longest seasonal migration, a round trip of more than 2000 km from winter range in Yukon's boreal forest to summer calving grounds on the Beaufort Sea coastal plain. Denali National Park, Alaska, USA.

Svalbard reindeer (*Rangifer tarandus platyrhynchus*). This short-legged subspecies, endemic to Svalbard's Arctic islands, is the smallest reindeer in the world and the most northerly herbivore mammal. It is estimated there are as many as 10,000 reindeer on the islands. With global warming and milder winters, the population is increasing with longer access to plant food. Svalbard, Norway.

Ungulates that live on islands tend to be smaller than those that live on the mainland. This allows more individuals to subsist on the same limited space and food supply, and thus to maintain higher genetic diversity and population viability. Reindeer are no exception, as shown with the small short-legged Spitsbergen subspecies (Rangifer tarandus platyrhynchus). The island dwarf is in the foreground, the mainland barren-ground form is behind.

Reindeer and Caribou

The reindeer of Eurasia became caribou in North America. The species has circumpolar distribution, primarily on the tundra and with the subalpine and alpine habitats in the northern fringes of the taiga. There are also populations of reindeer and caribou which have become forest dwellers. In winter, while living in forests, woodland caribou feed primarily on tree lichens, which are easily accessible. There is no need to fight for the food and female woodland caribou neither bear nor have use for antlers. By contrast, female reindeer and caribou on the tundra and in alpine areas subsist on ground lichens, which cannot be reached without digging pits in the snow. To defend such craters, both sexes need and have antlers, which they use against rivals, especially young bulls that would otherwise take the food. Male reindeer carry the longest antlers of all the deer family. The species is exceedingly fleet-footed for the long seasonal migrations between northern calving grounds and southern wintering areas.

Modern humans eventually displaced Neanderthal man and occupied all of Eurasia, before moving into North America. In the terminal phases of the last glaciations, people began to follow and herd reindeer, an industry still pursued in northern Eurasia. In North America, barren-ground caribou became the mainstay of native people living inland away from the coast. Reindeer occupy the high Arctic desert of Eurasia, including portions of Greenland. Here, and on Svalbard, reindeer grow much smaller, to even diminutive size. The largest and most primitive subspecies are the southern woodland caribou which may face extinction.

Reindeer became important to the people who settled in northern Eurasia some 40,000 years ago. They invented a sophisticated way of precisely intercepting migratory reindeer, killing them in large numbers, then saving the meat and fat as a long-lasting staple food. Having stored food to fall back on, these northern hunters began to decimate other herbivores that were essential for the existence of Neanderthal people.

Bugling wapiti (*Cervus elaphus canadensis*). Among living deer, the largest antlers are found on the reindeer among the Old World deer and the wapiti/elk among the New World deer. Jasper National Park, Canada.

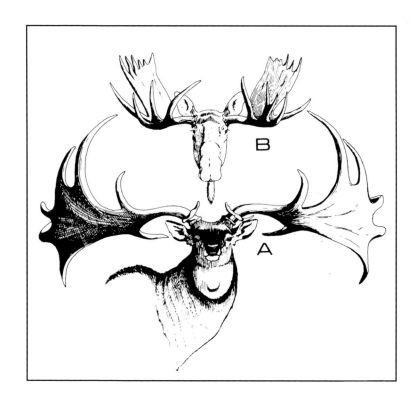

The "showiness" of the Irish elk (A) is evident in comparison with a large Alaska moose (B). Both species are of similar body size, but the Irish elk carried twice the antler mass. Although the spongy bone of its antlers didn't impair their effectiveness as weapons, their great breadth and weight made them unwieldy in combat. They were used mainly for visual display. Cave paintings point to a strongly marked, showy pelage on the neck and face of bulls.

Irish Elk, Wapiti and Alaska Moose

The Irish elk (*Megaloceros giganteus*) with its 4 m span of antlers is not an elk. It belonged to an old branch of deer with sub-species, large and small, scattered all throughout Europe and Asia. Nor was it exclusively Irish. Ireland boasts many well preserved skeletons of stags that fell through thin lake ice and drowned. Irish elk, like modern reindeer, escaped from predators by running out onto ice-covered lakes. Females, lacking the huge antlers, may not have depended so heavily on ice for escape, thus accounting for the lack of such skeletons in lakes. The Irish elk also found safety from predators by early detection and high-speed endurance running. This species was the most highly evolved runner among the deer family, had very big eyes, typical of fleet-footed plains dwellers, a ribcage to hold large lungs and heart and huge body proportions. The enormous antlers of the stag also indicates a life on the plains rather than in forests.

Since newborns had to follow fleet-footed mothers they were born large. The mother produced abundant amounts of rich milk resulting in the calves growing quickly to survival size. The larger antlers of mature males were more conspicuous in courtship of females. The largest antlers indicated superior feeding and physiological food-processing abilities which resulted in big calves and a maximum of rich milk. The palmed antlers of these plains dwellers, like those of moose, were set at an angle to reflect light thus attract breeding females. We can be quite certain that, like most Old World deer, this species would have advertised loudly with rutting calls. However, once a bull paired up with a cow, we can be quite sure courting couples would have been silent and secretive as moose tend to be. Anything else would attract the ever-hungry and all too eager predators.

Bull moose have bilobed antlers with huge palms that function as shields, rimmed with dagger-like tines. Although the antlers of some modern moose are over 200 cm wide, and those of some extinct species were even wider, the bull's neck is powerful enough to overcome the leverage of such broad weapons and drive the tines into an opponent or wrestle against the opponent's antlers. By contrast, the Irish elk developed antlers that were up to twice as wide. This meant the antlers of an Irish elk exerted about twice as much leverage against a bull's neck compared to a moose but the Irish elk's neck was weaker. So Irish elk with its ornate trilobed antlers, with their 4–8 tines, were less effective as weapons than as visual display organs functioning to impress females. Displaying, instead of fighting, works where females commonly have the final say in choosing a mate. Cow moose are notoriously choosy about their mate and it's not always the biggest bull or the winning fighter that gets chosen. Among living deer the longest antlered are the reindeer and the wapiti or elk. As expected, these are also among the most highly evolved runners of their respective subfamilies. At the European end of the mammoth steppe lived the last and least known of the gigantic deer, a giant wapiti far larger than the Irish elk. It is known as Owen's cave stag (*Strongyloceros spelaeus*) named in honor of the great British paleontologist Richard Owen.

The Irish elk was different from any moose. Although it had the largest antlers of any deer its body was not proportional. An ancestor of our moose, the broad-fronted elk (*Cervalces latifrons*), was even larger. It attained gigantic size about a million years ago in northern Eurasia. Although it stood about as high at the shoulder as big Alaska bull moose, it had shorter legs and thus a much more massive body. It was about twice the mass of an Irish elk. Not only was it less evolved in its legs than modern moose, it also had more primitive antlers with a narrower spread than those of the Irish elk. Its rostrum

resembled that of modern deer rather than that of modern moose which is adapted for feeding under water in lakes. Like the Irish elk, its teeth and nose were small, indicating it was more a foliage feeder and not as dependent on browsing as today's moose. It evolved at a time when Pleistocene glaciations were twice as common and winters were less severe than today. It migrated from Siberia to America, where it became the stag moose (*Cervalces scotti*). Its evolution was shaped by tremendous predator pressure which confined Cervalces to the huge shallow proglacial lakes or inland seas. Its hooves were larger than those of a moose. It could presumably escape predators by running better on mud, floating muskeg, through swamps and could outswim predators.

The extinct stag moose (Cervalces scotti) *being chased by a giant short-faced bear* (Arctodus simus). *This moose was as large as the largest modern Alaskan moose and had much more complex antlers. It was a long-legged trotter with large, widely splaying hooves providing traction on ice and better support for foraging in the shallows of the immense proglacial lakes that dotted the interior of Pleistocene North America. Both animals died out at the end of the last Ice Age, about 10,000–12,000 years ago.*

Left: Alaska moose with impressive dewlap (*Alces alces gigas*). Moose have bilobed antlers on short beams making the tines effective weapons and the palms effective shields. The Irish elk evolved with a weaker neck to support its more ornate trilobed antlers with 4–8 tines and wider beams rendering them less suited for combat than impressing females. Denali National Park, Alaska, USA.

The Alaskan moose (Alces alces gigas) is the largest living New World deer. Its body size and shoulder height matched those of the giant short-faced bear (Arctodus simus). One of the largest bears ever, it became extinct along with other ice age giants following the last glaciation.

Short-faced Bear, Brown Bear, Grizzly and Polar Bear

The Pleistocene was a time of giant bears. About 2.6 million years ago, North and South America were joined at the Isthmus of Panama, forming a land bridge. The North American predatory short-faced bear was quick to cross into South America and found a bonanza of prey with few and inefficient mammalian predators. South America's flora and fauna had evolved in isolation and dominant predators were large tyrannosaur-like "Terror birds," at least one of which, Titanis, managed to establish itself in North America. The South American giant short-faced bear (*Arctotherium angustidens*) grew into the largest land predator of the ice ages. The bear was twice the mass of a bull bison. There appears to have been good reason for its immense size. South America was home to giant prey, ground sloths reaching the size of elephants, rhino-sized toxodonts, soon to be joined by mastodons that crossed from North to South America. In addition there were indigenous large herbivores such as the camel-like Macrauchenia, big armored glyptodonts and pampatheres which were soon joined by horses, tapirs, deer and camels from North America. The giant bear was thus pitted against abundant large prey leading to its rapid increase in size. However, this family of bears began shrinking once the saber-toothed tiger Smilodon also crossed the isthmus and increased in size. As the South American short-faced bears shrank in size they became more vegetarian. Only one species survives today, the small, shy, largely vegetarian spectacled bear of the Andes (*Tremarctos ornatus*) and while South America's unique fauna was hit hard by animal invaders from the north, it was given the final blow by modern humans.

Left: Brown bear (*Ursus arctos*).The biggest brown bears in North America are found on Kodiak Island, Alaska, where males can weigh up to 680 kg. The largest known ice age land predator was the South American giant short-faced bear (*Arctotherium angustidens*). Reconstructions of its skeletons suggest that it may have weighed between 1500 to 1800 kg. Rising on its hind legs, it would have towered 3.3 m above ground. Lake Clark, Alaska.

Alaska Brown bear catching spawning sockeye salmon. A large dominant bear can catch and eat more than 30 salmon per day. Katmai National Park, Alaska, USA.

North American short-faced bears also grew large in a rich and diverse fauna as they were forced to compete with invading South American as well as Siberian predators. The result was a fauna dominated by giant predators with the northern short-faced (*Arctodus simus*) as the largest of three tremarctine bears. It was also the largest carnivore in North America, with big males pushing 900 kg, females were half that size. Claw marks left by the bear reached 4.5 m above ground. The adaptive plasticity of short-faced bears is illustrated by the contemporaneous Florida "cave bear", a big 300 kg bear, specialized as a herbivore! The short jaws allowed a much

higher biting force by the canines than did the elongated jaws of brown or black bears. The canines were also large. It appears that Arctodus grabbed and hung on with a jaw-grip of exceptional strength. He was a long-legged speedy runner. American predators of the time were remarkably specialized, as were the prey escaping or fighting them off. With their large size and powerful bite, *Arctodus simus* probably took over the kills of other predators. The bear was a strict meat eater, assertive but not very intelligent. Many of them were trapped in tar pits and caves, perhaps as scavenging herbivores. Similar accumulations of brown or black bears bones have not been found elsewhere.

Polar bear (*Ursus maritimus*). Polar bears diverged from brown bears about 150,000 years ago and adapted to seal hunting on the Arctic Ocean. Exceptionally large male polar bears may approach 800 kg. Hudson Bay, Canada.

Polar bears (*Ursus maritimus*) are larger than brown bears and adapted to preying on seals on the ice of the Arctic Ocean. Exceptionally large polar bear males may exceed 800 kg. The new brown bear ancestors were probably predators on the mammoth steppe, where it abutted onto the sea ice. This happened during the severe Riss Glaciation. In Europe, Deninger's bears ballooned into the cave bear (*Ursus spelaeus*), about the same time that Neanderthals were evolving there. Those cave bears, like grizzly bears today, probably exploited the root beds of alpine sweetvetch (*Hedysarum alpinum*) also known as Eskimo potato. Sweetvetch forms dense root beds in deep glacial silt (loess) close to glaciers. They can be long and thick and taste like a cross between carrot and parsnip. It is likely that the silt and loess bed, also attracted steppe marmots (*Marmota bobak*) and ground squirrels which could fatten up predatory bears prior to hibernation. Cave bears were were well suited to digging with massive front paws and shoulders and large, long finger claws. Brown bears, grizzly bears and black bears can also grow in size on a diet of salmon. While grizzly bears entered America late, black bears are native to North America. They evolved under severe predation and became very intelligent. Native North American species, such as black bears, coyotes, mountain lions, deer and pronghorns have thrived since the last ice age. But their Siberian counterparts — e.g. grizzly bear, gray wolf or elk — which entered North America after the megafaunal extinctions, are all too vulnerable in modern times.

American bison (*Bison bison*). The surviving species of American bison is not what would have been seen on the North American Plains as late as 15,000 years ago. Today's bison is a dwarf compared to its giant ancestor (*Bison antiquus*) with its huge spread of horns. Alaska, USA.

American Bison

Bison are the very last large-bodied (i.e. megafaunal) survivors of the great post ice age extinction that swept North and South America. Other large-bodied species which we think of as eminently American — e.g. moose, elk and grizzly bears — are East-Siberian immigrants that entered North America along with humans after the old native megafauna collapsed and became extinct. The only North American ungulates to survive that wave of extinction were smaller; the white-tailed deer, actually an ancient species and probably the oldest deer species in the world; the black-tailed deer, a west-coast derivative of the whitetail; the pronghorn antelope, actually not an antelope at all but an old lineage of ruminants confined to North America; the little peccary in the south, another ancient American ungulate with considerable species diversity. Among the carnivores that survived were the black bear, cougar, coyote and some earlier gray wolves that had persisted south of the huge Laurentide Ice Sheet which buried much of North America as far south as what is today Chicago and Toronto. The American bison one sees today is not what existed only 15,000 years ago. Today's bison is a dwarf. His giant ancestor (*Bison antiquus*) with its huge spread of horns shrank rapidly during and after the melting of the Laurentide and Cordilleran Ice sheets.

Bison developed from fairly small south Asian relatives long before the ice ages and then spread into cold climates. They became members of the cold-adapted ice age mammoth steppe fauna along with mammoth, woolly rhino, horse, camel, elk and reindeer. They spread to North America from Siberia following the mammoth steppe — a biome that stretched during glaciations from what is today Great Britain right across northern Europe, Asia, North America and Canada's Arctic islands. Bison entered North America late in the ice ages during the severe Penultimate Glaciation about 225,000 years ago. Simultaneously, in Africa our species (*Homo sapiens*) evolved at the same time as Neanderthal man evolved in Europe. It was also then that Deninger's bear evolved into the European brown bear and cave bear and that brown bears evolved into polar bears on the northern coasts of Eurasia and North America. In North America the ancestral bison evolved into the huge long-horned bison (*Bison latifrons*) which later gave rise to the ancient bison (*Bison antiquus*). Its horns could have spread to over 2.5 m. It was the largest bison ever.

*Modern bison (*Bison bison*) compared with the large predecessor ancient bison (*Bison antiquus*).*

Pronghorn (*Antilocapra americana*). Of all the large North American ice age mammals this is the only prairie species to survive the last extinction. Montana, USA.

Bison of the Eurasian mammoth steppe were a favorite target of Neanderthal hunters. They were subsequently hunted by the ancestors of modern people including ancient hunters in North America, especially after they had exterminated mammoth, ground sloths and mastodons. After contact with the Europeans, North American native peoples declined rapidly due to death from European diseases or by genocide. Bison multiplied into the huge herds that made them so famous. As these herds grew, fragments of North American native populations changed culture drastically when they adopted the European introduced horses as an aid to buffalo hunting. Mounted warriors were exceptionally successful against the invaders from Europe. The humiliated U.S. Army responded by trying to exterminate the bison. Food scarcity kept native warriors effective and dangerous. The bison extermination was indirectly financed by the market in buffalo hides which the U.S. Army fostered by establishing a secure transportation system around expanding railway lines. Bison, as a significant free-living species, was wiped out by 1885. A few of the famous wood bison survived in northern Canada along with a handful in Yellowstone National Park.

Muskoxen

Muskoxen are the lone survivor of a number of related large- bodied and large-horned ice age species, such as the shrub-ox (*Euceratherium collinum*), an American bison-sized, long-legged and large-horned form which did not survive contact with humans. Another was the large American forest muskox (*Bootherium bombifrons*), also big-horned and longlegged and a long-term survivor of the severe predation imposed by the diverse, specialized large North American predators before humans arrived. It was extinct 11,000 years ago as were most large-bodied North American species such as columbian mammoths, five groups of ground sloths, several species of horses, camels, llamas, pronghorns, stag moose, giant short-faced bear, saber tooth and scimitar cats, dire

wolf, and American cheetah. The muskoxen's natural range is today restricted to Arctic Canada and Greenland. However, it has been reintroduced successfully to sites in Alaska, Siberia, Sweden and Norway where it once was native. For over a million years the muskoxen inhabited the mammoth steppe and entered North America from Siberia during the severe Riss/ Illinoian Glaciation.

Muskoxen live in an extreme high arctic environment taking advantage of the short but intense growth of vegetation in summer to restore their bodies from the severe demands of the past winter, to grow new hair and to fatten up for the coming winter and reproduce when milk production can benefit from

Muskoxen were reintroduced to Dovrefjell from East Greenland in 1947 and 1953. Today approximately 250 muskoxen and 500 wild reindeer inhabit Dovrefjell National Park, Norway.

Bull muskox skull. A clean skull with horns can weigh up to 12 kg. Axel Heiberg Island, Canada.

plenty of vegetation. Muskoxen can store large quantities of fat throughout their body. They feed on sedges and grasses as well as low-growing forbs and dwarf willows. Because they consume tender arctic sedges, filled with sugars and proteins, muskoxen meat is a gourmet quality food and is currently sold at high prices by Canadian native corporations.

Currently, Banks Island in Canada enjoys the highest population of muskoxen, about 60,000 strong. The mammoth steppe biome was eventually replaced with acidic taiga and tundra during the melting of the continental glacial ice. In this

new biome, the muskox was more vulnerable to human hunting, as were the woolly mammoth, woolly rhino, steppe bison and horses. The vulnerability of muskoxen increased due to their tendency to protect themselves from predators by forming a ring, an effective tactic against wolves and felids but not against humans with primitive weapons. Killing an adult muskox was rewarded with 180-400 kg of tasty marbled meat and a superlatively insulating coat of long light, woolly hair. Only the vastness of the Arctic and its inhospitable conditions for human existence have saved the muskoxen from extermination.

Left: Bull muskox with cows and calf. For over a million years muskoxen inhabited the mammoth steppe. Earth's most extensive biome glaciation stretched from the British Isles across northern Europe, Asia, North America and Canada's Arctic islands. Seward Peninsula, Alaska, USA.

Coyote (*Canis latrans*). Native to North America and a close relative of the gray wolf. Great social flexibility and ubiquitous food habits saved coyotes from extinction during the ice age. Canada.

Ice Age Cats and Dogs

During the wave of postglacial extinctions the big losers were the cats and the big winners were the dogs. The big cats were almost completely eliminated or severely reduced in distribution much to the benefit of wolves, coyotes and jackals. There was a cause and effect relationship. The multitude of big cats, big bears and large hyenas very likely kept the big and small wolves in check — just as Siberian tigers apparently do to this day in Manchuria. That's why the tiger is tolerated and favored by native hunters and trappers. There were many large cats in the late Pleistocene. In the lower latitudes of North America there were two species of saber toothed cats, the highly social Smilodon a specialized killer of elephants and mastodons and the fast running dirk-tooth cat which was probably a gut-spiller, running up to prey and using the sharp, broad teeth to rip open

Left: Gray wolf (*Canis lupus*). The wolf crossed into North America over the Bering Land Bridge 125,000 year ago. Canada.

the flank allowing the guts to spill out tearing big blood vessels with death following quickly.

There were also lions in America, true lions but half as large as their African brethren. There were also mountain lions and the closely related American cheetahs that specialized in running down medium-sized prey. Big-bodied jaguars lived in the south and the Siberian tiger briefly was found in America but did not last. Eurasia retained the lion, tiger and leopard, at least until modern times when these large predators were greatly reduced or exterminated regionally. Canids did much better by virtue of their much higher reproductive rates, greater social flexibility and ubiquitous food habits. This may have saved wolves, coyotes and jackals from extinction but did not save the big American dire wolf of South American origin which managed to attain a rather modest distribution in warm climates. The African hunting dog, also a warm climate species, wasn't saved either.

The gray wolf was the biggest winner in the great post-glacial extinction of large mammals in America and Eurasia, where it was free to disperse and reproduce, only limited by its food supply, until the animal provoked intensive retaliation by human hunter-gatherers. In some areas, such as Greenland, the struggle between the two was such that there were large areas with people but without wolves, and vice versa. Wolves could easily prevent travel by dog sled. Archaeological sites without evidence of wolf scavenging suggest a mysterious absence of wolves. That might be explained if native people targeted wolves which are most vulnerable as pups in a den.

In Eurasia wolves were historically considered a curse. Not only were wolves blamed for severe plundering of livestock and wildlife, but also for the spread of pathogens, especially the rabies virus and hydatid parasites. Being bitten or even scratched by a rabid wolf's teeth was fatal. So much was

Arctic wolf (*Canis lupus arctos*). Young male babysitting pups. The white arctic wolf, possibly a distinct subspecies, ranges Canada's Arctic islands and northern Greenland. Its primary prey are muskoxen and arctic hare. Ellesmere Island, Canada.

rabies on the minds of medieval hunters that a 1717 German encyclopedia on hunting explains in detail how to determine from the tracks if a wolf is rabid. Today, a hasty search for medical help and vaccine can save rabies victims. Hydatid disease is caused by accidental ingesting eggs of the dog tape worm. This can happen to hunters and trappers handling wolf pelts, but nowadays a more likely source is the feces of domestic dogs that ate the lungs or livers of deer or livestock infected by these tapeworm eggs. These eggs grow in deer or livestock, or unlucky humans into large cysts in the lung or liver, which can be lethal when they burst, generating anaphylactic shock.

In Eurasia wolves killed thousands of people, yet such was not the case historically in North America. This is explained by the fact Native and colonizing Americans were always armed. Not only did Natives traditionally kill wolves, especially pups at dens, but hundreds of thousands of wolves have been killed by tens of thousands of Euro-Americans since the early 1800's. Wolf extermination was encouraged by bounties, as well as the trappers' own experiences with wolves spooking wildlife, destroying fur in traps or killing sled dogs. In addition to being trapped, wolves were killed by aerial poisoning programs, conducted by predator control officers, to halt losses inflicted on livestock. With wolf numbers low, there was so much wild prey for the remaining wolves, there were few wolf attacks on livestock, disease-threat was low, and attacks on humans unheard of.

Unfortunately, American wolves and coyotes will both target and attack humans under conditions of food-scarcity or habituation via garbage feeding, or by deliberate taming and feeding by visitors to parks. Even well fed wolves or coyotes, conditioned to humans, will target humans, especially children. Fortunately, circumstances favoring wolves attacking humans are exceedingly rare. The scarcity of attacks on humans by wolves in North America has nothing to do with the "nature" of American wolves, but everything to do with conditions that keep wolves away from humans. Lone wolves readily form liaisons with domestic dogs or coyotes. The Eastern Canadian coyote is a recent hybrid species from eastern wolves and invasive western coyotes.

Mountain lion or puma (*Puma concolor*). Closely related to the cheetah, these cats specialize in ambushing and running down medium-sized prey, especially deer. Widespread in both North and South America. Canadian Rockies.

Northern fur seal (*Callorhinus ursinus*). Beach master surrounded by his harem. Pribilof Islands, Alaska, USA.

CHAPTER TWO

Marine Mammals

Northern Fur Seal

Fur seals are close relatives of sea lions. Whereas the Southern Hemisphere has several fur seal species, the Arctic has only the northern fur seal. Mating battles can be spectacular when the males defend harems of females against other males on specific island beaches. The males may outweigh females fivefold. That's an indication of the severity of sexual competition which takes a heavy toll. While males live about 10 years, females may live over 25. A female's heaviest reproductive cost is raising a pup to weaning age. After giving birth and giving the pup a head start she must go hunting on the high seas for up to a week in order to feed and produce enough rich milk.

The relatively large flippers of fur seals provide exceptional agility in the water, a great advantage for catching prey and evading predators such as sharks and orcas. Fur seals feed on fish, squid and krill. While females feed during the mating season, males fast. Fur seals evolved on offshore islands free from terrestrial predators and did not develop an instinct to flee from danger on land. They did not flee, even when sealers entered their island-based breeding colonies. They were clubbed to death for their exceptionally valuable fur and their populations declined globally. They were saved by the remarkable 1911 Fur Seal Treaty, the first international wildlife treaty which included the United States, Great Britain, Russia and Japan.

Northern fur seal. The stout, long whiskers on this young seal are used in the water for sensing prey and predators. Pribilof Island, Alaska, USA.

Pacific walrus (*Odobenus rosmarus divergens*). Bull showing its long ivory tusks which can reach 100 cm. Wrangel Island, Russia.

Walrus

Grotesque giant mammals with huge tusks, horns or antlers inhabited northern latitudes throughout the ice ages and beyond until humans exterminated all but a few species. One that we failed to exterminate, though not for lack of trying, is the walrus, as odd a gigantic creature as any. Big bulls, at 1200 kg, weigh twice as much as the next largest pinniped, the Steller's sea lion. The huge tusks of walrus males and females are unique. Walrus are covered with what may be the toughest, thickest hide of all marine mammals. It can withstand the attacks of orcas, sharks and polar bears. Yet this massive hide can be flooded with blood for cooling, turning walrus pink, or drained of blood, turning a walrus ghostly white. The huge fat reserves of walrus suggest they gorge when food is abundant between long periods

Right: Atlantic walrus (*Odobenus rosmarus rosmarus*). Mother with calf on ice floe. Svalbard, Norway.

of scarcity. Their food is primarily clams and mussels. An adult walrus can eat 50–80 kg a day and it may take 8–10 hours to consume that much. They feed underwater at depths up to about 70 m, standing on their head and using their specialized mouths to suck clams out of their shell with enormous force. The quaint mustache apparently help walrus to locate food on the ocean floor. The accumulated masses of fat serve as insulation, but also as fuel for migrations. Between long bouts of swimming they rest on floating ice floes.

In the wide open spaces of land and sea concealment is difficult. To minimize predation of the young they are kept as long as possible within the mother's body. The young are large at birth and quickly able to escape from attackers. Escape capability is further developed through a rapid growth by feeding the infants copious amounts of rich milk. When young are threatened by a predator, the mother aided by other adults, defends the young. In terrestrial large herbivores this anti-predator strategy is associated with huge tusks, antlers or horns. In fact, the larger the father's antlers, the larger the baby at birth and the richer the mother's milk. The walrus is no exception. Baby walrus weigh a very substantial 64 kg at birth. Walrus milk is among the richest among pinnipeds and the mother suckles her baby for two to three years while protecting it ferociously. She carries it on her back or herds it ashore when orcas arrive or herds it into water should polar bears appear. If the calf calls for help its mother and other adults respond immediately. Male walrus may carry calves to safety tucking a young between their tusks and broad chest. Should the mother be killed another female may adopt her baby. Living in groups greatly enhances safety, something common to other large mammals living in wide-open spaces. There is no place to hide in the open ocean. It has worked well enough for walrus to survive even human hunting.

Steller's sea lion (*Eumetopias jubatus*). A large male barks at a female to keep her in his territory harem. Pacific coast, Alaska, USA.

Steller's sea lion (*Eumetopias jubatus*). Females, having hauled out on slippery rocks, lose their foothold in the waves of a rising tide. Kenai Fjords National Park, Alaska, USA.

Seal and Sea Lion

The marine environment was also colonized by early terrestrial predators. Relatives of bears evolved into seals and sea lions, while freshwater and marine otters evolved from the weasel family. All marine forms outgrew their terrestrial relatives. Unlike whales and sea cows, seals and marine otters are not totally aquatic, but spend some of their life on land or ice where they reproduce and may molt their skin. Although there are some 33 species of seals alive today, over 50 species are found in the fossil record.

While close to shore, on ice and in shallow water, prey can still hide to escape predators. But on the open sea, the only place to hide is among other animals, which is one reason why sea lions and other marine mammals travel in large congregations. If detected, the chances of being taken are high only at the periphery of the group, whereas individuals in the center are reasonably safe. So are individuals of at least average speed and agility; the slow and clumsy are more likely to be caught. Simply travelling as a group continuously at speed, makes it difficult

Harp seal (*Phoca groenlandica*). Mother returning to nurse her fastgrowing whitecoat pup. Gulf of Saint Lawrence, Canada.

Harbor seal (*Phoca vitulina*). Mothers with young. This seal has a worldwide range in the Atlantic along the Norwegian coast, Svalbard, Iceland, Greenland and the east coast of Canada's Arctic. Prince William Sound, Alaska, USA.

for predators to find or pursue the group. Prey also protect themselves by using auditory signals outside the predator's hearing range. Little wonder great white sharks focus their attention on sea lions when they are stationary, breeding in rookeries and producing lots of fat for clumsy and unwary pups.

Evolutionarily seals are highly successful. They are distributed globally. Siberia's Lake Baikal, the deepest freshwater lake on earth, hosts the Baikal seal, weighing barely 45 kg. Large seals prefer cold water. While most feed on fish and marine invertebrates a few, like the Antarctic leopard seal, feed on penguins and other seals. In turn, seals are preyed upon by polar bears, orcas and sharks. The primary attraction is their fat not their meat. After digestion of protein rich meat, clearing the kidneys of nitrogenous waste requires considerable water with low salt content, a resource that is difficult and costly to metabolize in the marine environment. Polar bears get their water from the chemical reaction that breaks down fat. The

primary prey of polar bears are the small ringed seals that live under and within winter sea ice. Ringed seals are also a very important prey of Inuit hunters. The seals are shot where they are hauled out onto the ice or skillfully speared at breathing holes in the ice. Inuit also use a specialized boat — the umiak — to hunt swimming walrus, seals and whales of all sizes.

Large populations of harp and gray seals off Canada's east coast were exploited commercially for hundreds of years without much controversy until the late 20th century. The clubbing death of baby seals with sweet, large-eyed faces caused animal protectionists to cry out in dismay and organize campaigns against the commercial killing of seal pups. Their campaigns included protesters joined by world celebrities on the ice for sensational front page news. While some seal harvest off Canada's east coast does continue the clubbing of baby seals was banned.

American river otter (*Lontra canadensis*). This aquatic mammal is a close relative to the sea otter. Resident in subarctic Alaska and Canada but not on the Arctic coast except Hudson Bay. The Eurasian otter (*Lontra lontra*) is rare in Fennoscandia but more common along Norway's west coast. Yellowstone National Park, Wyoming.

Sea Otter

The sea otter is the youngest marine mammal, making its appearance only five million years ago. Although it is among the smallest extant marine mammals at 45 kg it is the largest otter species, except for the long extinct African bear otter. Nevertheless, the sea otter is more adapted to marine life than the seals because it does not need to haul out on shore to reproduce. It is also one of the few animals that use tools. It uses rocks to dislodge mussels or break clams and sea urchins. Where sea otters are abundant they can reduce the numbers of sea urchins enough to prevent them from over grazing their habitat destroying the kelp forests. The sea otter differs from other marine mammals as it does not rely for insulation on fat, but on the air trapped in the exceptionally dense fur. Their fur made them so valuable to early explorers that they were hunted to near extinction.

Left: Sea otter (*Enhydra lutris*). Harriman Fjord, Prince William Sound, Alaska.

American River Otter

Not a marine mammal but a close relative of the sea otter. The river otter can be found along coastlines where it feeds on small fish, crabs and other invertebrates. However, the little otter is not fussy and will eat whatever small living thing it can catch, be it fish, insect, crustacean, amphibian, mammal or fowl. They may travel in groups. They are not particularly shy in part due to short-sightedness as their eyes are better adapted to underwater vision. These sleek, lively semi-aquatic weasels are very playful and a joy to observe. Their fur is dense and water repellent and has historically been highly valued, including by native people who also hunted them for food. River otters are social animals and can be tamed as pets. Fishermen in China regularly used another otter species to catch or trap fish.

Humpback whale (*Megaptera novaeangliae*). A great winged humpback breaches in the coastal waters of Alaska, USA.

Humpback Whale

The humpback whale's Latin name Megaptera means "great wings." The huge flippers can measure up to 5 m in length, a sharp contrast to the whale's slim appearance. The long, narrow pectoral fins are always white on the ventral side but the dorsal side can also be white or in different shades of black. Humpbacks are found throughout much of the Northern Hemisphere's Arctic Ocean as well as south into the Bering Sea, coastal Alaska and on to Hawaii. It is estimated there are at least 80,000 humpback whales worldwide. The males range in length from 15 to 16 m and weigh about 36,000 kg.

When modern genetics researchers investigated whales they got a surprise — genetically, whales are close relatives of pigs and hippos. Whales are thus a branch of the deer, cattle, giraffe, chevrotain and camel families. Some hippo relatives apparently began to exploit the rich intertidal zone and in time evolved into seafarers resulting in a lot of species taking advantage of many rich feeding opportunities in the oceans. Some whales evolved into grazers of the ocean plankton, mainly small crustaceans. Size ranges up to the humpback and giant blue whale. Others specialized as fish predators. These include several small marine and brackish water species such as the harbor porpoise and dolphin. River dolphins even invaded the major rivers like the Amazon, La Plata, Ganges and Indus. The largest predatory whales are the orca and sperm whale, which prey on fish, squid and other marine mammals.

Like a sea monster, a humpback explodes out of the sea creating a brilliant cascade of water. Alaska, USA.

The humpback's average tail span is 5 m. In adult whales the fluke's lower edge is a scalloped pattern. Alaska, USA.

Around the end of the last ice age the continents were swept with massive extinctions of large animals — a trend which continued during historic times on the oceanic islands. Deprived of carrion from terrestrial megafauna, gigantic scavenging birds, including the California condor became extinct. In inland habitats the condor survived only on the Pacific coast where there continued to be a steady supply of carrion from marine mammals which did not suffer extinction. Dead whales, sea lions and seals kept washing up along the beaches of California and kept the condor alive. Not until modern times did man pose a real threat to the ancient ecosystems of the oceans.

Whales appeared 50 million years ago. The baleen whales, the largest creature ever, would not exist had it not been for the ice ages starting at the South Pole. These enormous whales evolved over some 34 million years, taking advantage of the ice free, nutrient rich ocean circling the South Pole in summer, producing an enormous abundance of shrimp-like prey. The whales continued fattening up until the polar oceans froze over in winter. In summer the whales withdraw to warmer waters where they fast for months and reproduce. Arctic waters are home to the northern right whales, both the Pacific and Atlantic species, as well as to the closely related bowhead whales. These large baleen whales are adapted to surface feeding on plankton. All are highly buoyant due to their large fat reserves. Early 17th century whalers quickly noticed such whales did not sink when killed and were thus the "right whales" to take as their precious fat and baleen could be retrieved. Unfortunately, that popularity almost did these whales in. Even stringent recent protection has not led to noticeable recovery of the northern Pacific and Atlantic forms. In the Antarctic, southern right whales did somewhat better, and so did the arctic bowhead whales.

"Thar she blows" the whaler lookout would traditionally hail after spotting a surfacing humpback blowing out steaming pear-shaped white vapor from its blowhole. The vapor can reach a height of 6 m making it visible from a long distance. Alaska, USA.

An orca "spyhops" rising partly out the water for a better look while showing its many teeth, about 56 in total. Each tooth is about 76 mm long and 25 mm in diameter. Alaska, USA.

Orca or Killer Whale

Some orcas prey on other marine mammals including seals and sealions. Predation occurs both in the open ocean and where their prey haul out on beaches and ice floes. In the Antarctic, precisely coordinated orcas sneak up on ice floes where Weddell seals are resting, then swamp the ice floes washing seals into the ocean to their doom. Seals and sea lions becoming aware of orcas may beach themselves but inexperienced ones easily fall prey when orcas come out of the water to grab them. Porpoises developed sound communication outside the range of hearing of orcas, apparently as an anti-orca adaptation. Yet not all orcas prey on marine mammals; some populations favor fish.

Orcas or killer whales are the "wolves of the sea." They are pack-hunting predatory dolphins that occur

Orca breaches in the coastal water of Inside Passage, Alaska, USA.

in all oceans. The packs are matrilineal families, each of which displays individual hunting habits that are passed on from old to young. Consequently, food habits and hunting techniques are highly diverse between pods. Orcas off the west coast of Canada have been the most closely studied whales. Researchers found genetically distinct sub-populations, characterized by different hunting habits; the Residents, fed primarily on fish and squid; the Transients, which were wide-roaming feeders of marine mammals and the large offshore Pelagic Pods fed primarily on schooling fish but also on marine mammals and sharks. All three types are genetically distinct, indicating the cultural differences are ancient.

Similarly, in Antarctica, four different types of killer whales are recognized, each not only genetically distinct, but different also in ecology and hunting habits. These may well be differences at the species level for cross breeding between types has not been detected by analyses. These feeding specializations, powerfully reinforced by genetics, suggest successful feeding strategies are based on complex, specialized knowledge that can only be acquired by imitation for long periods of juvenile development within supporting pods. It suggests orcas have little tolerance of exploration or innovation that does not guarantee quick returns on the precious energy invested.

Left: Orcas (*Orcinus orca*) swimming at the surface show their forceful strength reaching speeds in excess of 55 kph, making them the fastest of the whales. Alaska, USA.

Beluga (*Delphinapterus leucas*). Whale group with young calf. Lancaster Sound, Nunavut, Canada.

A curious beluga "spyhops." Arctic Ocean, Canada.

Beluga or White Whale

The beluga is a relatively small, white arctic whale that lacks a dorsal fin, is exceptionally fat and presents a highly developed system of echolocation. All these attributes are adaptations. The absence of a dorsal fin allows belugas to swim under the sea ice (ice-hugging) when killer whales appear; the latter has a high dorsal fin which hinders hunting under the ice blanket. Dependence on ice-hugging for protection may be why belugas have not evolved as faster swimmers. Also, belugas have an exceptionally tough hide, another adaptation for scraping along the underside of ice flows when in danger. Their large fat stores protect them against both cold and periodic food shortages. Their highly developed sense of echolocation allows them to hunt in turbid river estuaries where they congregate in summer. Belugas trapped in ice may fall victim to polar bears, their only predator other than orcas.

Narwhal (*Monodon monoceros*). Aerial view of five males swimming near the water surface. Baffin Island, Canada.

Narwhal

The narwhal is a small arctic whale closely related to the beluga. It is characterized by a long, helical, ever-growing "tusk" that protrudes lancelike from its head. The tusk is formed by the left canine tooth. Like the beluga, the narwhal spends a lot of its time under the arctic ice floes and lacks a dorsal fin. Yet ecologically the beluga and the narwhal are totally different with the narwhal being prone to deep dives and feeding in deep water. The diagnostic feature of the narwhal, the tusk, is longest in males and appears to play a role in obtaining access to breeding females.

Narwhal. Tusking males compete for dominance. Baffin Island, Canada.

Polar bear (*Ursus maritimus*). The long, muscular neck and small head are adaptations for searching out the deep breathing holes seals make in the ice. The small ears are a result of acclimatization to the cold arctic environment. Hudson Bay, Canada.

CHAPTER THREE

Lords of the Arctic

Polar bear

No animal symbolizes the Arctic more than the polar bear. Not only modern audiences are in love with it; so too are the Native people that live in the Arctic. In this they do not differ from indigenous peoples globally, who lived with bears, including our ancestors dating back some 40,000 years. Bears have always captured the fears and dreams of humans. This is reflected in rich mythical stories but also in folk medicines where bear fat and bear parts played a large revered part — so revered that bears are still killed globally for the sake of "medicines" like dried gall bladders and the healing properties of fat and paws. While polar bear fur is the best insulation known to man, the fur of other bears is not far behind. When Inuit hunters hunch over a seal's breathing hole in the ice, they settle down on polar bear fur patches that keeps them from freezing. The Greenland hunters wear pants of polar bear skin as nothing else lets them endure extreme cold temperatures in adequate comfort allowing them to concentrate on hunting.

Polar bear claws are short and sharp, adapted for travel and climbing on ice. The grizzly bear's long claws have adapted to digging in dirt and gravel. Hudson Bay, Canada.

Inuit hunters revere polar bears and consider them spiritual beings with a soul that needs to be appeased. If hunters kill a polar bear, they will forego further killing for days in order to allow the soul of the bear to return to its ancestors with the hope that it will tell them how well it was treated and that its soul was freed and given precious gifts. People also tend to be captivated by the anatomy of bears as the skinned carcass eerily resembles that of a human. Also, bears can stand, even walk, on two legs or sit and scratch their tummy much like we do.

The polar bear is the biggest land predator in the Arctic and indeed in the world. When sparring, they look like formidable fighters. Hudson Bay, Canada.

Adult polar bears practice play fighting on the shores of Hudson Bay, Canada, while waiting for the ice to form. The bears spend lots of time sparring, testing an opponent's strength without killing. Hudson Bay, Canada.

The Inuit tell tales of bears shedding their skin when in a shelter and putting them back on again when going outside. Bears, they tell us have spirits that shamans can acquire as a high gift from the bears themselves. Respectful treatment of polar bears is a natural consequence. In our modern culture there is still a lingering respect of bears as symbols, "The Russian Bear" or a "Bear Market," and as jolly characters in children's books, such as *The Berenstain Bears*, or as lovable actors in ancient fables. If we look back even further, we discover how in our Western culture the ancient Greeks and Romans were infatuated with bears and how richly bears were woven into sacred tales.

Emerging from the icy sea in the Svalbard archipelago. This polar bear needs to shake off the water, or it will quickly turn to ice.

With a rotating head twist and a shake, the polar bear sends thousands of water droplets flying in all directions. Svalbard, Norway.

A polar bear female with her yearling cub along the shore of Hudson Bay, Canada.

Polar bears play a rich part in the religion of northern native people. Bears also play a part in religious tales and practices universally. Consider for instance the ancient bear sacrifices of the Ainu people of Hokkaido, Japan. A bear cub, whose mother is killed, is raised like a human child for two years and then killed with arrows, its blood is drunk and its skull and skin are wrapped around a spear and made into an object of reverence.

This young cub has learned to hide under her mother when another bear approaches. Hudson Bay, Canada.

In the Arctic polar bears were traditionally hunted with dogs. The dogs not only found the bear, but distracted it sufficiently to allow hunters to finish it off with a spear or with arrows. Natives had a use for every part of the carcass. The fat was eaten or burned as fuel along with the fat of seals or whales. The liver, however, was discarded. Due to its high A-vitamin content, the liver is poisonous to people and dogs.

Pregnant females are the only polar bears that hibernate. The well-insulated thick pelt conserves heat.
The body temperature of a resting polar bear is about +37°C. Hudson Bay, Canada.

Polar bears are derived from East Asian brown bears.
Consequently, the two species readily hybridize. Yet wild hybrids are rare as the preferred habitats of both species differ drastically. When polar bears retreated northward along the Pacific coast of North America during the last deglaciation, they bread extensively with brown bears shown by mitochondrial-DNA of ancient polar bear mothers. Polar bears evolved during the unusually severe Riss Glaciation some 130,000 years ago, which is the same period of glaciation during which we developed as *Homo sapiens* in Africa. Our sister species the Neanderthals, also evolved in Europe during this period along with other notable creatures like the cave bear, woolly mammoth and giant bison.

When too warm, bears lie down and stretch out anywhere on snow or ice. Hudson Bay, Canada.

Had there been less buildup of massive glaciers that drew water from global circulation during the Riss Glaciation, there would have been no outburst of rare species. A normal glaciation would not have forced coastal brown bears onto marine ice where they evolved into polar bears. Nevertheless, these early polar bears did so well that they grew into giants exceeding the size of current bears. Subsequently, polar bears evolved in an ongoing manner by natural selection to become ever more efficient predators of ice-bound seals. The primary food of polar bears are common ringed seals but they will also opportunistically consume other prey such as young walrus, baby beluga whales and narwhals trapped in ice. Polar bears will eat whatever else they can find including stranded whales, fish, birds, caribou, bird eggs, kelp, berries and human garbage. However, polar bears thrive when seals are abundant and the bears quickly consume only the fat from their prey. When numerous bears scavenge a stranded whale or walrus they form a dominance hierarchy. Lower ranking bears must signal submission to more dominant ones before being allowed to share the carcass.

During the summer bearded seals haul out on small ice floes for easy access to water and better protection from hunting polar bears. The bearded seal gets its name from the long whiskers which are used as feelers to locate clams, crab, shrimp and other molluscs in the sediment on the ocean floor. Svalbard, Norway.

Left: Bearded seal (*Erignathus barbatus*). This is the biggest seal found in arctic and subarctic waters. They have long white whiskers and thick claws are used to scrape through the ice to make breathing holes and escape routes. A bearded seal weighs between 200–425 kg and can grow to 2–2.5 m in length. Svalbard, Norway

Polar bears are master seal hunters. After a kill, the tough sealskin is peeled back and discarded along with meat and bones. Normally only the energy-rich blubber, up to 7 cm thick, is consumed — if the bear is quick enough to do this before a bigger rival arrives to steal the prey. The wings of a glaucous gull can be seen in the lower right corner. Svalbard, Norway.

During the polar bear's peak hunting season, from March to June, each bear kills on average one bearded seal or ringed seal per week. What the bear doesn't eat is eagerly consumed by scavengers such as arctic fox, glaucous and ivory gulls. Svalbard, Norway.

At the beginning of November polar bears leave the coast and head out on the now ice-covered bay to hunt for ringed and bearded seals. Hudson Bay, Canada.

Left: Fresh polar bear tracks crossing ice floes towards Bell Island.
The walking speed for a polar bear is about 4 kph. Franz Josef Land, Russia.

Northern lights dance over Prelude Lake. Northwest Territories, Canada.

Polar bears mate in late April or May but the fertilized eggs implanted in the uterus do not grow until fall, this is called delayed implantation. A pregnant female enters or digs her den in September/October and gives birth there two months later, normally she has two cubs weighing about 1 kg each. They remain in the den until March or April when the mother leads them out onto the ice where she can catch seals. The cubs depend on her for two to three years, according to the severity of the environment.

Right: As the sun sets, polar bears roam the frozen sea ice of Hudson Bay searching for seals.

Polar bears have a circumpolar distribution although the majority exist in Canada. After their evolution during the Riss Glaciation they survived the exceptionally warm interglacial period that followed, when ocean levels rose five meters higher than they measure today and hippos splashed in the Thames River in England. Those early polar bears were less specialized than today's animals, which became ice-bound super predators only during the height of the last glacial ice age, the Wuerm/

Wisconsinian Glaciation, between 22,000 and 18,000 years ago. Since sea ice is vital to polar bear survival, the loss of sea ice is a legitimate cause for concern. Currently, polar bears are largely holding their own and enjoy protection under an international treaty. The long history of wildlife management teaches a clear lesson, wildlife thrives where it is "used" not where it is strictly protected.

Grizzly (*Ursus arctos horribilis*). Female with newborn cubs. Mating season runs from late May through July and peaks in mid-June. The cubs are born beginning of January or early February. Banff National Park, Canada.

CHAPTER FOUR

Bears of the Northern Hemisphere

Grizzly Bear

There were at least three major waves of immigration by Eurasian brown bears (*Ursus arctos*) across the Bering Land Bridge at the end of the last ice age. The first wave occupied inland habitats where they competed with the last of the Pleistocene mega carnivores and became fierce grizzly bears. They colonized as far south as Mexico. The grizzly has a reputation for nastiness harking back to the fact that a grizzly mother on the open plains cannot send her cubs up a tree for safety, like a black bear mother can. A grizzly mother defends her cubs against predation by wolves and other bears even if the odds she faces are formidable. She might also protect them from a human who seems dangerous, even if the person actually means no harm. Mistaken defensiveness is most common where grizzlies are hunted. On the other hand, hunted grizzlies tend to avoid humans except near sources of prime food (e.g. an elk carcass or a salmon stream). So whether the net result of hunting is to increase or decrease risk to humans varies on a case-by-case basis. At the end of the ice age, when Alaska's coastal ice finally melted, the last wave of ursine immigrants occupied the newly available coastal habitat — they are called brown bears like their Eurasian relatives.

Grizzly/brown bears feed on a great diversity of foods, some of which they dig out such as the nutlike root lumps of lanceleaf springbeauty (*Claytonia lanceolata*), or the root tubers of northern sweetvetch (*Hedysarum boreale*). Grizzly bears also dig for ground squirrels and marmots which are fattest shortly before the rodents hibernate. But bears also like garbage, which decades ago they were fed in national parks to attract tourists with cameras. When policies changed, these bears

Black bear (*Ursus americanus*). This bear is a cinnamon color phase variation of the North American black bear. The colors vary in this species from black to white. A brown black bear is sometimes mistaken for a grizzly bear. North America.

were supposed to immediately switch to a diet of just natural foods. However, adapting took years, as did trial and error development of "bear proof" garbage cans. Meanwhile, grizzlies kept obtaining garbage wherever they could. They are smart and persistent. This cost the lives of many bears, especially those that left the national parks and foraged in human settlements. With the "back to nature" movement, bears and humans interacted on park roads and humans were punished for feeding bears.

Grizzly (*Ursus arctos horribilis*). Compared with coastal brown bears, grizzlies do more digging for underground plant tissues (e.g. roots and tubers) and prey (e.g. ground squirrels and marmots). Therefore grizzly claws tend to be shorter — one reason why grizzly tracks are more likely to be mistaken for black bear tracks. Banff National Park, Canada.

Black bear (*Ursus americanus*). This species is only distantly related to brown or polar bears. North American black bears split from Asian black bears and came to North America before the great ice ages. Banff National Park, Canada.

Black Bear

Black bears came to North America before the major ice ages. Their intelligence rivals that of chimpanzees, a consequence of living for at least two million years surrounded by the extreme predators that characterized North America's ice ages, like the sabre-toothed cat and the giant short-faced bear. Black bears, which have adapted to the forest, climb trees for safety. Being able to escape up trees rather than having to face enemies on the ground, makes black bears less dangerous compared to grizzly and brown bears. However, that might not be true of the one Canadian black bear population which lives on the open tundra in the Torngat Mountains of Labrador, a territory they share with hibernating mother polar bears. As long as black bears are well fed, they are remarkably peaceful. Predatory attacks by black bears are carried out primarily by males. Failure to fatten for hibernation can mean danger to humans. Good crops of huckleberries and blueberries lead to rapid fattening and peaceful bears, while berry crop failures may make the bears seek out alternate food sources, including orchards, groceries and garbage in human habitations. That's when you need to be "bear smart" — a task not to be underestimated, as bears outsmart humans again and again.

Brown Bear in a pine forest near the Russian border. Since 1970 Russian bears have encroached upon the Finnish taiga. Kuhmo, Finland.

Male brown bear (*Ursus arctos*). The brown bear descended from the Eurasian etruscan bear (*Ursus etruscus*) and spread into Europe about 250,000 years ago. Kuhmo, Finland.

European Brown Bear

European and Asian brown bears are close relatives of the North American brown and grizzly bears. Asian brown bears venturing beyond the tree line and exploring arctic ocean shores gave rise to the polar bears two glaciations ago. Deninger's bear, an early ancestor of the brown bear also created the cave bear which survived only until the end of the last ice age and is now extinct. Brown bears are opportunistic generalist, feeding on wide range of prey, carrion and plant foods. During the birth seasons of moose, red deer or reindeer, bears are especially active hunting newborns. They also feed on salmon, clams and marine mammal carcasses that wash up on shore, as well as livestock.

Brown bears on the arctic tundra may travel far enough north to reach to the Arctic Ocean. On rare occasions this leads to hybridization with polar bears. These hybrids may become more common if global warming raises the temperature in the Arctic. However, polar bears survived the last interglacial period which was much warmer than our current interglacial. Oceans were then five meters higher than today. Nevertheless, humans have altered the polar bear's environment so much that they may no longer be able to survive a major rise in sea level. Bears are very adaptable. Unfortunately, this leads them to prey on livestock, reindeer herds included, and they display remarkable cunning in raiding livestock and avoiding people. While normally peaceful, brown bears have killed people who persisted in following them, for instance in freshly fallen snow, to their secret winter den.

Alaska brown bear (*Ursus arctos*) hunts for sockeye salmon. Lake Clark, Alaska.

Alaska Brown Bear

Alaska brown bears are the giants among brown bears because they exploit the riches of salmon runs, fertile shoreline meadows and berry crops. When the massive salmon runs go up Alaska's rivers, brown bears descend to feed on fish. It is a spectacle and a tourist attraction. So rich is the feed at times that bears, gorged on salmon, take only the choicest portions of the fish, such as the fatty skin and the brain. The bears parcel out the choice fishing spots among themselves on the basis of dominance. While the lure of the salmon makes the bears very tolerant of humans, they have killed overly assertive or careless humans.

Spawning sockeye salmon swim against the current in Adams River, Canada.

Alaska brown bear. "The bum shake." Lake Clark, Alaska.

Alaska brown bear "The head shake." Lake Clark, Alaska.

Polar Bear

The polar bear, the king of the arctic ice, evolved to thrive on the blubber of seals. However, like many other species of bears, they are all too often attracted to the garbage in human habitations such as in Churchill, Manitoba, located on the shore of Hudson Bay. Here, garbage is now collected and stored in bearproof facilities. Very determined polar bears are stuck into bear prisons where they must wait until the sea ice returns and they can resume hunting seals. Still, enough polar bears hang around town to thrill tourists. Game Wardens are on call for any reports of threatening situations. Residents never lock their car doors thus adding to available quick and safe escapes for anyone wandering through town who may meet a polar bear. Soon, the hungry bears will disappear for the winter season and be gone searching for their primary prey, the ringed seal.

Polar bears have become an icon for conservation. They are a spectacular beast, while their cubs are droll beyond words.

A female polar bear takes her three-month-old cubs from the maternity den to Hudson Bay sea ice. Females den many kilometers inland to avoid meeting cannibalistic males. Wapusk National Park, Canada.

Polar bear and ringed seal (*Phoca hispida*). These bears depend on seals so much that their respective numbers rise and fall together. Svalbard, Norway.

Where people and polar bears rub shoulders, such as in the Manitoba town of Churchill on the Hudson Bay, a flourishing tourist industry has developed. While films and videos of polar bears playing with sled dogs were flashed around the globe, so too were pictures of orphaned polar bear cubs raised in zoos. Yes, bears do touch us, especially as they can stand and walk about briskly on two legs. It is easy to grasp why native people see bears as mythical creatures or why they appear in our fairy tales. In reality, however, polar bears lead a hard life as seal hunters on the ice. If life were not so demanding they would be neither white nor excellent swimmers. The watchful eyes and ears of seals have shaped them. Polar bears are being continually and mercilessly tested by their prey. Little wonder those cute baby bears need their mother's rich milk, her hunting skills and some two and a half years of learning before they can succeed on their own.

Polar bears and ringed seals live in a reciprocal relationship. Polar bear predation tends to lower ringed seal numbers, whereas a rise in seal abundance also tends to increase bear abundance. The beautiful white coat of newborn seals in the north comes courtesy of polar bears. In the Antarctic, with no terrestrial seal predators, newborns are brown. And that speaks to the hard and dangerous life lived by bears. Females den many kilometers inland to avoid cannibalistic males. On the long march back to the sea she must avoid not only males, but also grizzly bears and wolves. When she arrives, if ice conditions are not favorable for hunting seals, mom and babies may starve. Less than half of cubs survive their first year and few of those are weaned at one and a half years of age, for most it is two and a half years. Few female cubs reach sexual maturity before four years and for males the age is six years. However, polar bears are long lived and they can live more than 20 years. The best friends of the polar bear are still native peoples, who hunt them but cherish and thank them for the meat, hide and the adventures that give rise to the "bear lore." People who love to watch bears in the wild can also contribute a lot to their conservation.

Gray wolf (*Canis lupus*). Wolves self-domesticated about 12,000 years ago by exploiting refuse heaps outside villages, as human populations multiplied with the advent of agriculture. Canada.

CHAPTER FIVE

Hunters of the Arctic Tundra

Wolf

**The gray wolf benefitted from the Pleistocene extinctions that
swept North America and Eurasia about 11,000 years ago,**
eliminating enemies and competitors — the big cats, predatory
bears and giant dire wolves. The exception is Manchuria, where
Siberian tigers (*Panthera tigris altaica*) survived. Its presence
is favored by residents because the tiger eats wolves and
bears. Wolves have a high reproductive rate, are exceptionally
intelligent and are effective predators. Wolves are also the origin
of "man's best friend." Cute dachshunds, charming papillons,
dainty chihuahuas, massive St. Bernards, fast whippets and
showy poodles are all tamed wolves. Domestication began about
12,000 years ago along with the advent of agriculture. Farming
not only saved expanding human populations from certain
starvation and death, it also resulted in enough garbage to
support wolf packs. The packs that adapted best to this lifestyle
evolved into dogs. Humans found many uses for the new,
affable companion. This led to the spread of dogs worldwide.
There are today at least 525 million dogs globally. They serve
not only as loyal companions and reliable helpers, they are also
a food source.

A curious four-week old wolf pup taking a peek from the den.

Although the typical wolf coat is mainly gray with black and white markings, the coats come in many colors, from white to black and many shades in between. Canada.

Where wolves and humans are competitors, people have gone to great lengths to control wolves. In Greenland, in historic times, there were uninhabitable regions because of wolves. Where humans depended on resources not shared with wolves, like in coastal communities where wolf numbers were low for ecological reasons, wolves were looked upon more benignly. In Japan wolves destroyed deer and pigs that raided the precious field crops. However, when rabies broke out, it was the end of living together and they were exterminated by 1905. A rabid wolf was then always lethal and the animal spread not only rabies but also other deadly diseases. Europe's weaponless peasants dreaded the wolf because of its great skill in raiding livestock or killing humans. Red Riding Hood's story correctly reflects the wolf's cleverness. Medieval rulers put a lot of effort into exterminating wolves and whole villages cooperated to drive wolves into nets that stretched for miles. Where wolf numbers are low relative to prey abundance, wolves shun people and livestock and are harmless — unless they start feeding on garbage, lose their fear of people and start treating them as prey. A benign view of wolves in modern times allowed wolves to spread into populated areas and also enjoy protection. Unfortunately, such wolves are destined for genetic extinction through their hybridization with dogs. Lone wolves readily search out dogs even within suburbs.

Left: At birth, the iris of a wolf pup is dark and later changes to amber-yellow around the black pupil. Canada.

Eurasian lynx (*Lynx lynx*). Norway.

Lynx

Lynx are large cats highly adapted to northern taiga or boreal forests. In North America they primarily hunt snowshoe hares. Consequently, the great ups and downs in the cyclical numbers of hares also generates large ups and downs in lynx populations. The Eurasian lynx is twice the size of the North American lynx and has a larger range of prey, including forest grouse, roe deer and chamois. In Newfoundland, lynx are efficient predators on newborn caribou and moose. In medieval times their white meat was a delicacy only royalty could afford.

Canada lynx (*Lynx canadensis*). Canada.

Lynx are solitary hunters like all other terrestrial arctic predators except wolves. Lynx hunt by secret ambushing and instantly cut the spinal cord of prey as large as caribou calves. Unconsumed portions of the kill are hidden under a layer of moss or other vegetation. Such caches are virtually impossible for a person to detect with the naked eye and appear to be well hidden even from ravens. Carrion from other sources is normally avoided, unless fresh prey is unavailable. The better nourished the lynx is, the more young it produces. Like all solitary cats, lynx are very shy and are seen very rarely. They are mainly nocturnal.

Wolverine (*Gulo gulo*). Wolverine have dense, oily fur that is highly water repellent. Kamchatka, Russia.

Wolverine

Wolverine are the largest terrestrial member of the weasel family, as large as a mid-sized dog, but more muscular and bear-like. It has a reputation for ferocity, for it seldom flees from even much bigger enemies. Also, like other members of the weasel family, it may kill prey much larger than itself, such as deer or caribou. However, most of its food is carrion killed by other predators such as wolves, weather or accidents (e.g. avalanches).

The wolverine is a solitary animal and a great traveler, cresting the very tops of mountains. They occupy huge territories, with a male overlapping those of several females. Males may weigh twice as much as females. Wolverine have dense, oily fur that is highly water repellant and does not collect ice during winter from human breath. This makes it highly valued by Arctic people for trimming the hoods of parkas.

Right: Wolverine tracks in the Canadian Rockies. Largely solitary animals and great travelers. Wolverines sometimes crest very high mountain tops.

Red fox (*Vulpes vulpes*). The North American red fox is a descendant of the fine-haired, cold-adapted northern Siberian fox. Kamchatka, Russia.

Red Fox

Red fox occupy habitats from northern Mexico north to the southern fringe of the Arctic where it is replaced by its smaller cousin, the arctic fox. Only one species of red fox is recognized as circumpolar, but there are at least 45 subspecies. It is clearly a successful animal which can thrive even in suburbs and cities. It has a broad diet including berries and carrion, but also small mammals, birds and insects, ingesting over 300 organism species. North American foxes are descendants of fine-haired, cold-adapted northern Siberian foxes. They are specialists in detecting and pinpointing mice under the snow, because of their sensitive ears and catch the rodents with a long, arching and accurate jump. The fox caches the prey, rather than gorging. The light body enables them to jump long distances accurately and to escape predators.

When a fox caches mice in the snow it disguises the site. Then as it leaves the cache it walks backwards, erasing its tracks with the nose. Later after returning to finish the cache, the fox marks the empty cache with a drop of urine. When the fox next passes this site the smell of urine, combined with that of food, tells the fox that whatever meal was there is gone. Although red is the most common coat color of red fox, the fur can also be black, silver, platinum and amber in several dark variations and rarely even white. Fox fur is highly prized and the animal is often farmed. On one Russian farm, a famous breeding experiment was performed selecting the friendliest fox in each generation. This resulted in cute "domestic dogs" that were attracted to people rather than fleeing in panic, as red fox do where they have been hunted or harassed by humans. This provides clues to the self-domestication of wolves into dogs.

Arctic Fox

These fox find and catch small rodents the same way red fox do. They too cache excess food for future use. Although arctic fox eat a variety of prey, including some birds and young seals, their main prey is lemmings. Their normal litter is 5–8 kits, but they can exploit periods when lemmings are very abundant to produce even more kits. They have the largest litter of any arctic carnivore. This allows fox populations to grow quickly, compensating for losses during periods of near starvation when lemmings are scarce. Arctic fox are monogamous, territorial and live in large and complex underground dens.

Arctic fox (*Alopex lagopus*). Summer coat. Svalbard, Norway.

Foxes are highly successful small predators and the arctic fox is no exception. It has a wide circumpolar distribution. Due to its thick, dense fur and specialized circulatory system, it thrives in cold weather down to -70°C and is active year round. Its wonderful fur was avidly used by our ice age ancestors. Arctic fox prey not only on small birds and mammals but also on newborn seals, bird eggs and carrion left by polar bears and wolves.

Arctic fox (*Alopex lagopus*). Winter coat. Their keen sense of hearing enables them to pinpoint the locations of lemmings under the snow. Alaska.

Weasel and Marten

The smallest hunters of the Arctic and boreal forest belong to the weasel family. They are the marten or American sable which prefer mature coniferous forests and the larger fisher which is found in early succession forests. Both produce fur of exceptional quality, both were over-trapped, and both have responded well to conservation measures, including re-introductions where they had been extirpated. The smallest predators are the ermine or short-tailed weasel which overlaps with the slightly larger long-tailed weasel and with the smaller least weasel (*Mustela nivalis*) — which is the smallest carnivore of all and widely distributed in North America, Eurasia and North Africa. Its stubby tail lacks the black tip found in ermine. In the north they all turn white in winter and the beautiful white dense fur was always highly prized and used to decorate the robes and cloaks of kings and popes.

These small and ferocious hunters kill not only voles, mice, and small birds, but also rabbits and forest grouse much larger than they are. They rapidly explore nooks and crannies where prey may be hiding, including tunnels dug by squirrels under the snow. They are greedy feeders and not above accepting meat offered by the human hand and will boldly explore the inside of cabins in the woods. They can be trained to come when called and can quickly eliminate mice from a cabin. After making a kill, they may — just like cats after a difficult hunt — perform a "dance" during which they also toboggan over the snow, propelling themselves forward with rapid thrusts of the hind legs.

Short-tailed weasel or ermine (*Mustela erminea*). In winter this weasel turns white and is known as ermine both in Europe, Russia, Alaska and Canada.

Least weasel (*Mustela nivalis*) surrounded by wild wood anemone. Germany.

American marten (*Martes americana*). Marten prefer mature coniferous forest. The larger fisher (*Martes pennanti*) is found in early succession forest. Both produce fur of exceptional quality. Canada.

Barren-ground bull caribou (*Rangifer tarandus*). Caribou from the Bathurst herd east of Great Bear Lake during its southerly migration. Northwest Territories, Canada

CHAPTER SIX

Arctic Grazers

Reindeer/Caribou

Known in Europe and Asia as reindeer, and in North America as caribou, this is the most fleet-footed and hardy of all deer. Its fate is closely tied to that of humans in the north. Reindeer became abundant during the last glaciation and were hunted by modern humans as soon as they reached the cold interior of Eurasia. Humans learned to time the migrations of reindeer and hunted them so successfully that they developed a luxury economy based on the animal. They learned to conserve meat and fat to tide them over in lean times and to use reindeer skins with their exceptional thermal insulation. Food was so abundant that early northerners grew tall and athletic, with exceptionally large brains. Reindeer have remained important in northern Asia and America ever since, although they were domesticated only in Eurasia, never in North America. As other large mammals such as mammoth, woolly rhino, bison and horses were hunted to extinction, people began to following the reindeer herds. One still finds such reindeer cultures in Europe and Asia where herd owners keep the annual production for themselves by displacing or killing large carnivores that might prey on the reindeer.

Barren-ground caribou (*Rangifer tarandus*). Bull with antlers still in velvet. Denali National Park, Alaska.

Fall in the high country and home to moose, grizzly bear, caribou, Dall's sheep and wolves. A few stunted white spruce (*Picea glauca*) linger at the timberline before winter, in a sea of dwarf birch (*Betula glandulosa*) in deep crimson. Alaska Range, Denali National Park, Alaska.

Barren-ground caribou (*Rangifer tarandus*). Before rutting season in early September bulls shed the velvet leaving antlers stained with blood. Denali National Park, Alaska.

Kongsfjorden or Kings Bay near town of Ny-Ålesund. Seven national parks and 23 nature reserves cover two thirds of Svalbard's archipelago. Svalbard, Norway.

Spitsbergen

Spitsbergen — Norway's Svalbard archipelago consists of a large group of islands located well above the Arctic Circle between 74–81 degrees north latitude. The summer's arctic climate is short but enjoys significantly higher temperatures than other areas at the same latitude due to the warming influence of the Gulf Stream. Seven national parks and 23 nature reserves cover two-thirds of the archipelago protecting the largely untouched, yet fragile environment. The land surface of the islands is 60% glacial ice, 30% barren rocks and 10% vegetation.

At the end of the last ice age, 10,000 years ago, the Svalbard reindeer became genetically isolated from the mainland population and developed into the smallest subspecies of reindeer. Spitsbergen at its most northern point is only 1,100 km from the North Pole. The sparse vegetation has a very short growing season from late June to early October. Norway assumed sovereignty over Spitsbergen Islands in 1925 and the Svalbard reindeer were given protected status. At that time the estimated number was around 1,000 animals. There are no exact figures for the current population but believed to be around 10,000. Reindeer hunting is allowed for permanent residents only.

A Svalbard reindeer with new antlers still covered in velvet. Norway.

Alaska-Yukon moose (*Alces alces gigas*), the largest moose subspecies in the world. The maximum recorded measurement for Alaska-Yukon moose antler spread is 208 cm collected in 1958 at Redoubt Bay, Alaska. Denali National Park, Alaska, USA.

Moose

Moose are the largest living deer and have circumpolar distribution. They moved into North America across the Bering Land Bridge about 10,000 years ago together with elk, grizzly bears, gray wolves and humans. That was just after the collapse of the native North American fauna which had been dominated by giant herbivores and carnivores. Moose have evolved to exploit the young growth of shrubs and trees after a fire or flood, as well as wet sedge meadows and aquatic vegetation. Its odd shaped muzzle contains nasal valves that allow it to feed under water.

Lashing out with the powerful front legs or kicking with the hind feet is their defence against predators. The many broken and healed bones of wolves attest to the power of moose hooves. Moose tame readily if caught very young and have been used in ancient times as mounts, as beasts of burden and as milk producers.

A dominant bull with a magnificent bell or dewlap, an organ used during rutting season for holding and distributing urine-scent. Alaska-Yukon moose. Denali National Park, Alaska, USA.

Cow moose with calf. Moose have a high reproductive potential. They exploit the secondary growth after wildfire sweeps the coniferous taiga and when high quality food is abundant, cow moose frequently give birth to twins, and occasionally triplets. Under such conditions the calves reach early sexual maturity and breed in their second year. Denali National Park, Alaska, USA.

Moose mating season peaks in late September. Bulls and cows are attracted to one another, with cows noticeably preferring large bulls. They may even attack and chase off small bulls and rival cows. The rutting bull splashes its bell with urine-soaked mud while rolling and pawing in rutting pits. The bull's urine-scent is irresistible to cows. Denali National Park, Alaska, USA.

Moose country. Chugach Mountains, Alaska, USA.

Left: Bull moose in rut. The final velvet comes off from the top of the antlers. The back surface of the antlers is stained darker than the front, as it is more likely to come in contact with vegetation during trashing. This keeps the front of the antlers whitish and quite noticeable in the dim light of dusk and dawn when the bulls are most active. Bloody antlers just freed from velvet signal the beginning of hard, serious and dangerous competition for cows. The bulls have prepared all year for this. They must breed in the next six weeks or wait another year for a chance. Banff National Park, Canada.

Arctic Ground Squirrel

Arctic ground squirrel is widely distributed with ten subspecies in the Eurasian and North American Arctic. It prefers open landscapes, such as arctic and mountain tundra where it lives in large colonies. It is a true hibernator that burrows three feet down in sandy soil, builds an insulated sleeping chamber and stores food (leaves, seeds) for consumption after it awakes in spring. These squirrels stay in burrows from early fall to April with the females hibernating a bit earlier than the males. Arctic ground squirrels pack on huge amounts of fat before hibernation. A fattened animal will weigh close to one kilo. Native people prefer to eat ground squirrel in late summer when it is fattest. That's also when a grizzly bear may dig up whole burrow systems to catch these squirrels. Arctic ground squirrels are highly productive with litters that have up to ten babies indicating that juvenile mortality is high, probably due to predation.

Arctic ground squirrel (*Spermophilus parryii*). Native people prefer to eat these ground squirrels in late summer when they are at their fattest. The skins are used for mittens. Ivvavik National Park, Yukon, Canada.

Hoary marmot (*Marmota caligata*). This is North America's largest ground squirrel. Their heavy layer of fat attracts hungry grizzly bears in the high country. The marmots are true hibernators, spending seven to nine months a year sleeping in underground burrows. They range from Alaska and Yukon south throughout British Columbia's mountains. Banff National Park, Canada.

Hoary Marmot

Hoary marmot is the largest ground squirrel with the largest, fattest males pushing 13 kg prior to hibernation. Almost half of that weight is fat — which makes them a prized food for grizzly bears preparing for hibernation and for native hunters. The slightly smaller cousins of the hoary marmot in Asia and Europe attracted bears and human hunters for the same reason. Native hunters rendered the fat down and poured it hot over berries they had picked into bags made from marmot skins to preserve the berries. The meat of marmots was smoked to preserve it. The fat of Eurasian marmots is used to relieve rheumatic pain, for wound dressing and to cover burns or frostbitten skin. Marmots have been hunted as long as humans have shared their habitat.

Arctic hare (*Lepus arcticus*). The arctic hare is one of the largest living lagomorphs and can weigh up to 7 kg. It is distributed over the Canadian tundra, from the treeline to all of Canada's Arctic islands and the northernmost region of Greenland. It is an exceptionally fast and agile runner reaching a top speed of 60 km/hr. Banks Island, Canada.

Arctic Hare

Arctic hare is the largest hare, weighing up to 7 kg. It is found in the Canadian Arctic and Greenland, but also as far south as Newfoundland. These hares take shelter in burrows dug into hard snow, which insulates them from the outside cold. Several hares may huddle for warmth. While foraging, these animals occasionally form congregations, numbering in the hundreds. The arctic hare is fertile giving birth up to eight young per litter, a sign that it lives under severe predation pressure from arctic fox, red fox, wolves, lynx, snowy owl, gyrfalcon and rough-legged hawk. It is hunted by native peoples for its meat and its densely furred skin. It is exceptionally fast, reaching a top speed of up to 60 km/hr. Agility and a camouflage coat help it escape predators. In the far north hares stay white year-round. At the lower latitudes, where the snowshoe hare replaces the arctic hare, hares change from white in winter to gray-brown in summer.

Arctic hare. These social animals are only active at night. In late winter they gather by the hundreds on windblown slopes where they feed on dead vegetation, until everything is eaten, then disperse to new grazing areas. They are favorite prey of arctic wolves. Ellesmere Island, Nunavut, Canada.

Arctic hare in transitional coat from winter to summer.

Snowshoe hare (*Lepus americanus*). The hare's fur is still tan and brown on the face, back and sides, but will soon turn into pure white for winter camouflage. Denali National Park, Alaska, USA.

Snowshoe Hare

Snowshoe hares are famous for their cyclical abundance in the boreal forest, peaking every eight to 11 years. At peaks there may be over 600 rabbits per sq. km. They attract all sorts of predators — lynx, wolves, coyotes, goshawks and great horned owls. The reduced reproduction of hares, through severe predation and ongoing depletion of food, drives down the hare population and lowers the fertility of female hares, but also lowers the fertility of their offspring. Then, as the hares continue to decline so do the predators. However, at peak hare abundance, wolf packs have been seen feeding on hares and ignoring moose close by. As rabbits decline, wolves switch to moose and deer. Lynx, which are less effective deer predators may forego reproduction or even starve to death when rabbits are scarce. The fates of predators are linked to the fates of their prey.

Mountain hare (*Lepus timidus*). This species is distributed from Scandinavia to eastern Siberia but not in North America. It is also known as blue hare because the winter coat is not pure white. In the mountains of Norway and Sweden, the hare is found in alpine habitats. Scottish Highlands.

Mountain Hare

Cousin to North America's snowshoe hare, the mountain hare — also know as blue hare — is even more widely distributed. It breeds on taiga and tundra from the northern part of Sweden, Norway and Finland, east across Siberia from the Kola Peninsula to Kamchatka. Both species have adapted to polar and mountain habitats. They molt in the fall and the fur turns completely white except for the mountain hare's black ear tips and the tail which remains white all year. The mountain hare is the bigger of the two and can weigh 4 kg. The snowshoe hare is much smaller, 1.5 kg.

Collared Pika

Pikas are tiny relatives of rabbits and hares, living in rockslides and famous for "hay making." There are 30 species world-wide, but only two reside in North America, the collared pika being the northern most. Each pika defends its territory, where it gathers little hay piles in summer, food for the long winter ahead. Pikas do not burrow but depend on a warm microclimate within the rockslide.

Collared pika (*Ochotona collaris*). Although the pika does not hibernate, it thrives only in cold climates — making it an effective indicator species of the impacts of global warming in the lower alpine ecosystem. Denali National Park, Alaska.

Norway Lemming

This small rodent fills its prey niche in the arctic ecosystem for hawks, owls and foxes. Lemming suicide legends were reported centuries ago in Scandinavia. In 1855, Swedish archbishop Olaus Magnus wrote in his book, *History of the Nordic Peoples*, "that a sudden appearance of a legion of lemmings was likely due to their descending from the sky."

Norway lemming (*Lemmus lemmus*) hiding in dwarf birches at Flatruet, a 975 m high plateau in the Swedish mountains. Norwegian lemmings are endemic to northern Fennoscandia where they range from the mountains to the Barents Sea east to the Kola Peninsula.

Northern collared or snow lemming (*Dicrostonyx groenlandicus*). Snow lemming feeding on purple saxifrage. Found in the arctic regions of Asia, North America and the Arctic islands of Canada to northeastern Greenland. The fur is reddish in summer but turns white with the onset of winter. Greenland.

Arctic Lemmings

Lemmings are big, short-tailed, blunt-headed arctic mice found on the tundra of Eurasia and North America. They can be abundant when there is plenty of food. Their abundance tends to be cyclical, but irregular, peeking roughly every four years. They eat leaves, shoots, grasses and sedges as well as insect larvae. Unlike ground squirrels they do not hibernate but burrow underneath the snow blanket, searching for food. They also store dried grass during summer and build grass nests for the winter ahead. They are solitary and aggressive and they are quite visible on the tundra. Weasels, arctic foxes, arctic owls, jaegers and gyrfalcons prey heavily on lemmings. The predators reproduce quickly during lemming highs and suffer reproductive failure when lemmings are scarce. During peak abundance, when they run out of food, lemmings may move in search of better pastures. In Norway, narrow mountain valleys may channel migratory lemmings into rivers and lakes that are hazardous to cross. The occasional mass mortality led to the myth that lemmings commit mass suicide.

White-tailed ptarmigan (*Lagopus leucura*). In winter, ptarmigan feed on nutritious willow buds to keep warm and healthy. Banff National Park, Canada.

CHAPTER SEVEN

Grouse of Taiga and Tundra

Ptarmigan

Ptarmigan are well adapted to harsh winter environments. They are one of the unusual groups of birds that molt their body feathers and change color three times a year. In winter, they are pure white, except for their black eyes and beak. In snow, this plumage camouflage protects them from predators. You will see their tracks in the snow before realizing they are nearby. In spring, ptarmigan have a patterned plumage that blends into the varied vegetation, again to avoid predators. In summer, they molt to mimic the late summer plants in the alpine. The females incubate their eggs and thus have complete molts. The males do not visit the nests; consequently they can save some energy and retain some white feathers in the spring.

In winter, ptarmigan eat willow buds that protrude above the snow. In the mountains, they usually have to descend in elevation into valley bottoms where willows are taller than the snow depth. Despite the cold and apparent scarcity of food, ptarmigan actually put on weight in winter. The willow buds are so nutritious that the ptarmigan can stay in a warm and healthy condition. Moose also eat the willow buds and branches. How much ptarmigan reduce bud supply, and thus forage quality for moose, isn't yet known.

At night in winter, ptarmigan avoid the extreme cold by burrowing into deep snow where they sit insulated until sunrise brings warmth. To avoid leaving a trail that predators could follow by sight or scent, ptarmigan don't walk to a burrow site. Instead, they fly into a snow bank near sunset to hide overnight. This works well until spring, when the warmer days and cold nights can leave a hard crust on the surface of the snow. Ptarmigan have been known to break their necks on hard crust. It's not unusual for winter travelers to ski or snowshoe right over a bird hiding in the snow, then to be spooked when the bird suddenly explodes beneath their feet and flies away in a cascade of ice crystals over the frozen tundra.

Rock ptarmigan (*Lagopus muta*). Male in winter plumage with black tail feathers. Its call is a dry, crackling "garrr-gurrr-gurrrr." Swiss Alps.

The flaming leaves of dwarf birch and boarberry carpet the tundra in one spectacular display at the onset of winter. Point Lake, Northwest Territories, Canada.

Ptarmigan are the architects of the shrubs they eat. Willow buds are major winter foods for ptarmigan. In addition to nipping buds from the end of branches, ptarmigan can also break the new branch tips. In winter, the buds are reduced because of the depth of snow. Buds more than a few cm below the snow surface are so inaccessible to ptarmigan that only 3% of them are harvested by the birds. Ptarmigan forage mostly on buds up to 30 cm above the snow surface, eating up to 90% of the buds. Hence, nearly all growth of a willow shrub occurs below the winter snowline. This results in low, wide willows that tend to grow out rather than up. The short stature of ptarmigan-browsed willow benefits shrub alder, which is not eaten by ptarmigan. Shrub alder can thus outgrow and shade willow. The warming climate in the Arctic is causing willow and other shrubs to grow more rapidly. However, the benefit to ptarmigan is unclear, since climate change also affects the depth of winter snow and availability of willow branches and buds. Other species dependent on willow buds are moose and arctic hare. Ptarmigan have the advantage of flying to new areas with more buds, possibly leaving the mammals behind with less food to survive the winter.

Willow ptarmigan (*Lagopus lagopus*). During spring mating season, the male's breast, head and neck are liver red. Once a year from mid August into early September, willow ptarmigan molt and shed their liver colored feathers for completely white plumage. Northwest Territories, Canada.

Svalbard rock ptarmigan (*Lagopus mutus hyperboreus*). This rock ptarmigan is the only non-migratory land bird that resides permanently on the glacier covered islands of Svalbard's archipelago. Norway.

Rock and Willow Ptarmigan

Svalbard's rock ptarmigan is an endemic subspecies restricted to Svalbard, Bear Island and Franz Josef Land. This rock ptarmigan is the only non-migratory land bird that resides permanently on the glacier-clad islands of Svalbard's archipelago. Rock ptarmigan are the staple food of gyrfalcons on Hrisey Island off the north coast of Iceland. With no other predators on the island, ptarmigan numbers peak roughly every ten years. When ptarmigan are abundant, gyrfalcons nest on the island. Even though ptarmigan are the main prey of this large falcon, the falcon does not eat enough ptarmigan to reduce the population. The numbers appear to decline with lack of

vegetation, rather than because of predation. When ptarmigan populations are low, the gyrfalcons leave and nest elsewhere. In places where both rock and willow ptarmigan occur, gyrfalcons prefer willow ptarmigan. The reason for this preference is not clear; possibly because they are easier to catch or tastier.

Life span and number of young are linked in ptarmigan and in most other species of birds. Species with longer life expectancy have fewer young and those with short life expectancy have more young. Willow ptarmigan produce more young and live shorter lives than other ptarmigan. Rock ptarmigan produce

Willow ptarmigan (*Lagopus lagopus*). Male in aerial display over the Finnmarksvidda tundra, nesting habitat for willow ptarmigan among scrubby birch and willows. Norway.

Ptarmigan's nest with six eggs is well camouflaged on the alpine tundra. Ptarmigan have a short lifespan and live only one to three years in most cases. Alaska.

fewer young but live longer lives. White-tailed ptarmigan have both slow and fast lifestyles depending on where they are. In Yukon, they have more young but live shorter lives than further south in Colorado. Predation of nests by mammals and predation of adults by raptors such as gyrfalcons are major causes of mortality in these short-lived species. During the breeding season, gyrfalcons have higher nest success when there are lots of fledgling ptarmigan, which appear to be more vulnerable to this fast predator. Ptarmigan only live one to three years in most cases but produce an average of one to four young per year.

White-tailed ptarmigan. The nesting areas for this ptarmigan are above treelines in mountainous terrain. Climate change has created a particular challenge for this species. Jasper National Park, Canada.

White-tailed Ptarmigan

White-tailed ptarmigan on mountain tops are isolated from other suitable habitats. If the habitat changes, they have to move or die. Climate warming creates a particular challenge for this species. In Montana's Rockies, this species has moved 335 m upslope to cooler habitat in 15 years. The flocks of ptarmigan are less numerous in drier habitats and on steeper slopes. At the southern edge of their range in New Mexico, the species is particularly vulnerable. As the climate warms, they will eventually run out of mountain and disappear from one alpine area after another. The same may happen to willow ptarmigan

in Newfoundland where this species occurs in low densities. The weight of adult ptarmigan here declines with increased density, indicating that this island's food supply is limited for this species of grouse. Living in the arctic and alpine regions can be perilous with cold, wet weather possible throughout summer. Young ptarmigan must be very careful to stay warm while eating enough food to grow. Adults do not feed young ptarmigan; rather they feed themselves while the female watches for predators. All chicks in a brood will feed at the same time.

White-tailed ptarmigan. Ptarmigan take advantage of the natural protection of snow and will bury themselves deep into soft powder snow, which is good insulation against cold weather and wind. Banff National Park, Canada.

Male white-tailed ptarmigan display alone to attract a mate, not in leks like black grouse and capercaillie. Once the male attracts a mate he follows her, spending a quarter of his time displaying just for her, until she lays eggs. Displaying appears to have two advantages. First, it can ensure that no other male mates with her and when she lays eggs. Since eggs are laid every one to two days, each egg could be fertilized by a different male. By staying with her, he is certain that the clutch of eggs is his. Outside-pair copulations are rare in this species, compared to grouse species that mate at leks. The second reason relates to the risk of predation. Females spend more time foraging when males are with them, vigilant of predators. She does not need to better look around to see if a predator is near. By feeding carefully, she is able to lay more eggs and spend more time on the nest incubating the eggs, taking shorter and fewer times away from the nest, which in turn reduces the chance of detection by predators.

Hazel Grouse

Hazel grouse is one of the smallest members of the grouse family. This shy species occurs across northern Eurasia from central Europe and Scandinavia to Japan in moist coniferous woodlands. The species is suitably named since its distribution and abundance is tied to the density of alder and hazel shrubs. In winter, they eat the buds and staminate catkins of alders that are over 10 m tall and typically grow less than 15 m from spruce forests. Where agriculture clears the boreal spruce forest, the grouse disappears more than 100 m from the edge of the spruce forest. Fear of predators likely limits this species' willingness to leave the dense cover of spruce trees.

The trade-off between finding food and finding a mate and avoiding predators is illustrated by this species in winter. When not breeding, pairs often stay in their territory feeding near each other if they are far from cover, where both could watch for predators and can spend more time feeding and less time watching. Where cover is dense and alder catkins and buds are abundant, they feed alone. Sometimes they will feed near neighbors of the opposite sex, presumably hedging their options in case their own mate did not survive the winter. By spring, they want to be in their best habitat with a mate. In eastern Siberia more open forests with more food shrubs results in larger flocks in winter. These flocks can forage efficiently since there are more birds to watch for predators.

Female hazel grouse (*Bonasa bonasia*). The male can be distinguished by his black chin and throat. One of the smallest members of the grouse family. This species requires mature spruce forest mixed with some deciduous trees and an abundance of alder and hazel scrubs. Jämtland, Sweden.

Spruce grouse (*Falcipennis canadensis*). When approaching a female during mating season, the males expose swollen red combs, raising and spreading tail feathers. Banff National Park, Canada.

Spruce Grouse

This species may be misnamed based on its diet. In winter, spruce grouse eat mostly needles from lodgepole pine trees in Alberta, Canada. In summer, their diet is more varied and includes berries when they are available. In autumn, pine needles are only half of their diet since other plants are available before frost arrives. During this time, the grouse spend more time in the conifer trees. They are not forced there by deeper snow, rather they appear to increase the proportion of needles in their diet, gradually increasing the size of their stomach and intestines to survive on the poor nutrition provided by the pine needles. The size of their digestive system is mirrored in the size of muscles and organs which are larger in winter. Overall, the grouse are heavier in winter despite the poor diet. Some grouse move 500–1000 m between winter and summer habitats to find more favorable conditions.

Eurasian black grouse (*Tetrao tetrix*). Colorful male displaying at lek, an important mating area in early April to mid-May when hens visit the grounds. Suitable leks can contain small groups but up to 100 or more birds have been recorded. Bergslagen, Sweden.

Black Grouse

Black grouse is a lek display species; the males congregate in spring in a small area and the females watch from the periphery before choosing a mate. The males tear feathers from each other; those that lose the fewest feathers tend to be most successful at breeding. The females appear to be making the correct choices since successful males are more likely to survive over the next six months, apparently stronger than the losing males. The number of males in a lek and the size of the lek is important to the breeding success of males. Leks with more males attract more females, and despite the added competition from other males, males in larger leks are more likely to successfully breed with a female than males at small leks. A genetic study found that successful males actually have a more diverse genome, while unsuccessful males appear to be the product of inbreeding, or breeding with a relative. Some males appear to be Casanovas. Once a Casanova has mated with one female, other females are attracted to him and allow him to mate with them.

Eurasian black grouse. Two males on a lek fight over their respective territories in aggressive jump-fighting. Bergslagen, Sweden.

Western capercaillie. Female on display grounds competing with other females to mate with dominant male. A few days after being fertilized, females begin nesting and within 10 days lay a clutch of eight to 12 eggs. Jämtland, Sweden.

Capercaillie

In Scandinavia and likely elsewhere, the population cycles of three species of grouse — capercaillie, black grouse and hazel grouse — are synchronized with peak numbers approximately every six years. However, they select differently aged forests. Black grouse prefer young conifer forests up to 20 years old, hazel grouse inhabit mid-aged forests 20–25 years old and capercaillie occupy the older forests over 90 years old. Thus black grouse seem better adapted to post-fire landscapes which are avoided by capercaillie.

Left: Western capercaillie (*Tetrao urogallus*). Male in all his glory displaying on lek for females ready to copulate. The capercaillie is the largest member of the grouse family and can weigh up to 5 kg. They range from Scandinavia across northeastern Eurasia up to the northern limits of the taiga forest. Bergslagen, Sweden.

Rasing young is risky for capercaillie and hazel grouse. Typically, two-thirds of the chicks in the nests are eaten by mammal predators, particularly members of the weasel family and foxes. Most are eaten early in the incubation period (first half of May); and fewer later, possibly because more alternate food is available in the second half of May. These grouse benefit when small mammal prey increases. Fewer nestlings are eaten when mice, voles and lemmings are abundant for predators.

Male capercaillie display for females in groups called leks. The males typically do not participate in leks until they are four years old. In the first two springs, they move between leks presumably deciding where to display. Once they are mature and display at a certain lek, they return to that lek every spring.

Above: Snowy owl (*Bubo scandiacus*). Adult female flying over the arctic tundra looking for lemmings and voles. Varanger, Norway.

Right: Snowy owl. The male snowy owl is almost pure white with few speckled brown bars and spots. In winter, snowy owls from Alaska have been tracked south to the Canadian prairies. Alberta, Canada.

CHAPTER EIGHT

Northern Raptors

Snowy Owl

Snowy owls nest around the planet in northern treeless regions. In spring, they wander the Arctic looking for lemmings, their favorite food. Lemming numbers rise over several years, then crash, before increasing again in a four to ten year cycle. The owls have to search for areas with a high number of lemmings before they will settle in to breed. The male owl needs lots of lemmings to feed seven to 11 young and their mother — who feeds the young and keeps them warm. In low lemming years, snowy owls may reduce clutch size to no more than three young. They may also wander; for example one nestling owl tagged on Victoria Island in the Canadian Arctic was found 18 months later 6,000 km away on Sakhalin Island, Siberia.

In winter, snowy owls from Alaska have been tracked south to the Canadian prairies looking for an adequate winter food supply of small mammals, ranging in size from meadow voles to larger prey such as jackrabbits and grouse. Owls wintering in central Alberta come from as far way as Alaska, northern Ontario, Quebec and the arctic islands, all congregating for abundant food on the prairie grasslands.

Without sign posts to tell them how to find food, these owls must wander the northern parts of America and Eurasia looking for food in summer to breed and in winter to survive. One snowy owl was tracked from its winter home in southern Saskatchewan to northern Canada and then back to the same winter site, indicating they will revisit an area to see if food is still abundant before searching new areas. Standing over a half meter tall, these white owls can be seen perched on poles in grasslands during winter. The amount of dark flecking reflects the sex and age of the owls with young females having the most dark flecks and old males the least.

The snowy owl is built to withstand harsh weather. Their dense feathers have the same insulation value as the fur of arctic fox and the wool undercoat of Dall's sheep. However, to cope with severe arctic cold and wind, snowy owls need to eat four to seven lemmings per day. In the south, mice and voles are typically smaller than lemmings, so the owls need even more prey each day. Lemming populations fluctuate in cycles of three to four years in each area of the Arctic. Populations of small mammals in the southern parts of the owls' range fluctuate with even longer time periods. The owls travel widely looking for habitats with prey densities high enough to sustain them.

Short-eared Owl

Short-eared owl (*Asio flammeus*). Owls from Alaska have been tracked to central Mexico using small satellite transmitters and have been found nesting on oceanic islands such as Hawaii and Galapagos. Alberta prairies, Canada.

Short-eared owls wander the treeless arctic tundra and temperate grasslands looking for high populations of small mammals, especially voles and mice. Owls from Alaska have been tracked to central Mexico, using small satellite transmitters. In spring, none returned to Alaska; rather they stayed in Montana and Alberta where meadow voles were abundant, and the owls bred there. Others that nested in Alberta left at the beginning of winter despite high prey densities. They were tracked to Kansas, flying 500 km per night for four nights in a row; their autumn migration was over after four nights and 1900 km. Such flying abilities have resulted in this species of owl nesting on oceanic islands such as Hawaii and Galapagos as well as around the globe in the Northern Hemisphere and throughout southern South America.

As cattle graze prairie grasslands and tractors cultivate fields, the number of voles has declined resulting in declines of this once abundant species in North America and Europe. When food is abundant, these owls may nest as close as 500 m apart and forage over each other's territories to feed the numerous young. In winter, they may roost communally where mice and grasshoppers are abundant. Further north, when snow falls they will roost in conifers, or fly south to escape snow so they can catch mice more easily. Only 5 cm of snow is enough to move owls from their ground roosts to coniferous trees, possibly because these brown owls lose their camouflage in white snow.

Northern Hawk Owl

The hawk owl exists all across the Northern Hemisphere. However, their ecology varies between Eurasia and North America. In Eurasia, the hawk owl's livelihood is dependent on voles, among the smallest mammals in the boreal forest. Hawk owl breeding effort and success vary in synchrony with the three to four year cycles in vole density. In fact, the owls will roam long distances in search of areas with a high vole density, then breed in that location. By contrast, in North America the hawk owls eat prey ranging in size from voles to snowshoe hares, which are much larger. The most abundant prey makes up most of an owl's diet. This diversity of diet allows the owls to reproduce more frequently and benefit from the cyclic peaks of both voles and hares. However, if the cyclic lows for both prey occur at the same time, the hawk owls will leave that area and not nest until they have found higher prey densities.

The North American hawk owls are about six percent larger than European hawk owls, possibly related to larger prey. As its name implies, the hawk owl is an unusual owl. This species is diurnal and hunts more like a hawk than like other owls. It has a long tail for increased manoeuvrability, relatively long pointed wings for fast takeoff and flight, lack of silent flight, which is not needed in the daytime and lack of ear asymmetry needed by other owl species for listening for food in the darkness. All of these characteristics are similar to hawks, which also hunt in the daytime. Hawk owls prefer open forests where they can find trees for nesting and unforested meadows to hunt for prey. They nest either in a tree cavity, that was typically excavated by a large woodpecker or on the top of a broken tree trunk, where a hollow has been created in the rotten stump.

Northern hawk owl (*Surnia ulula*). Interestingly, the North American hawk owls are about six percent larger than European hawk owls. Alberta, Canada.

Female boreal owl (*Aegolius funereus*). This smaller northern forest owl needs tree cavities for nesting. Jämtland, Sweden.

Boreal Owl

This smaller northern forest owl needs a tree cavity for nesting and lots of voles for food. The tree cavities are typically made by larger woodpeckers such as black woodpeckers in Eurasia and flickers, three-toed and pileated woodpeckers in North America. The cavities of smaller woodpeckers are not big enough for this owl to raise six young per year. The density of voles in the northern boreal forests varies dramatically from place to place in a typically nine to ten year cycle. The variation between population density lows and highs can be as much as 200 fold. During lows in prey populations, these owls must move to find areas with abundant food. When prey population density is high, an owl doesn't need as much area to support its family; owl territory sizes decrease accordingly. Owl clutch size also increases.

Left: Boreal owl chick sits in the nest opening to the tree cavity made by a black woodpecker. Jämtland, Sweden.

Great gray owl (*Strix nebulosa*). Female flying to her nest site in a broken birch stump. Jämtland, Sweden.

Great Gray Owl

Great gray owls are a species of the deep woods. This large owl is densely feathered, like snowy owls, to cope with cold. Like many other species, their primary prey are voles. In winter, great gray owls are able to hear voles moving about beneath the snow and after a silent glide from their perch they plunge feet first into the snow with talons spread wide to clasp the unsuspecting vole.

When these owls hunt in natural grass meadows they mostly eat voles, but when they hunt in clear cuts they eat the larger northern pocket gopher. Pocket gophers spend most of their time tunnelling underground, eating plant roots. When they surface during the night they might attract the attention of a hungry great gray owl.

Like hawk owls, great gray owls sit silently on a tall perch listening and looking for prey. Whereas the hawk owl hunts mostly in the daytime, great gray owls hunt mainly in the evening and at night. Both species nest atop broken tree trunks. They are too large to nest in tree cavities like some smaller owls. The great grays will also use large stick nests built by hawks.

Right: Great gray owl. Female with newborn chicks. When these owls hunt in natural grass meadows they mostly eat voles, but when they hunt in forest clear cuts, as in North America, they eat the larger northern pocket gopher (*Thomomys talpoides*). Jämtland, Sweden.

Eurasian Eagle Owl

This is the largest owl species, weighing in at 4 kg. Its tall ear tufts contribute to what humans regard as a fierce demeanour. Whether that helps to ensure it has no natural predators remains unknown. In the wild, they can live up to 20 years and in captivity have lived 60 years. Its large size means that it can eat a wide variety of prey. In Mongolia, eagle owls eat mainly small mammals especially marmots and hamsters. Elsewhere this owl has eaten cats, dogs, foxes and even deer. It will also kill and eat other large raptors including northern goshawks, buteos and even peregrine falcons. In coastal areas ducks, seabirds and geese are consumed. One unusual prey are prickly hedgehogs, which are carefully skinned before being eaten. Sometimes cleaning up the environment has unintended negative consequences. When the elimination of rural garbage dumps in Finland reduced the number of rats, it eliminated a food supply for this large owl species. In the mid-1990s, loss of rats reduced owl density by two percent per year. In parts of Asia, its feathers are incorporated into amulets to protect children and livestock from evil spirits; its talons are used to ward off diseases.

Eurasian eagle owl (*Bubo bubo*). This is one of the world's biggest owls, weighing about 4 kg.

Great horned owl (*Bubo virginianus*). During a peak in snowshoe hare numbers, nest density of great horned owls also peaks, producing 2.5 young per successful pair. Alberta, Canada.

Great Horned Owl

Although this large owl is widespread in North and South America, its calls are poorly known. One study found five types of hoots, four types of chitters and two squawks that are used to proclaim territory, to greet a mate, to state that they are ready to breed, to announce they have delivered food to the nest and to beg for food. The purpose of some calls is unknown. In northern North America, breeding success is dependent on the abundance of snowshoe hares. The numbers of hares vary over a ten-year cycle. During a peak in hare numbers, great horned owls nest in high densities and produce 2.5 young per successful pair. When the number of hares crashes, many owls leave and those that remain will only produce about 1.6 young per pair. In the boreal forest, black flies are more than a nuisance to young owls; the flies can kill young by sucking blood and infecting them with a parasite. This effect is worst during times of food shortage. Unusual prey of this owl are skunks. As an owl kills and eats a skunk, the owl apparently ignores the skunk's smelly oily spray.

Rough-legged Hawk

This large arctic raptor has one of the broadest distributions in the Northern Hemisphere ranging from the treeline in summer to mid-latitudes of North America, North Africa, the Middle East and central Asia in winter. Despite its size, this hawk has a relatively small bill and feet suited to catch and kill its prey, lemmings and voles in summer, voles and mice in winter. The rough-legged hawk has huge wings to reduce its wing loading allowing it to fly slowly, or even hovering (wings beating like a giant hummingbird) or kiting (motionless sailing in the air), while it looks for prey. Both summer and winter they live in open treeless grasslands where their prey is accessible. Large flocks occur during migration. In winter several hundred may roost together, especially where food is abundant.

Rough-legged hawk (*Buteo lagopus*). Adult hawk migrating through southern Sweden. This large raptor migrates from the taiga down to mid-latitudes of North America, North Africa, the Middle East and central Asia.

Gyrfalcon, white-morph (*Falco rusticolus*). Adult falcon showing wet underfeathers. Over much of the gyrfalcon's range its breeding season is tied to the abundance of willow ptarmigan. Greenland.

Peregrine falcon (*Falco peregrinus*). Perched on an old tree stump. Falcon populations steadily declined due to DDT until the cause was documented and DDT was banned in most of the world. Scotland.

Gyrfalcon

Gyrfalcons, the largest species of falcon, nests on remote cliffs across the Arctic. From their high perches, they swoop down on ptarmigan, ducks and other birds. Gyrfalcon breeding season over much of their range is tied directly to the abundance of ptarmigan, the grouse-like birds of the Arctic. Gyrfalcons prefer willow ptarmigan, but if willow ptarmigan are not abundant gyrfalcons will eat rock ptarmigan. In coastal areas of the Arctic, gyrfalcons feed more often on waterfowl and seabirds. Gyrfalcons wait to nest until the ptarmigan start courting and the migrant waterfowl and seabirds arrive. When bird prey is not available and when lemmings, ground squirrels and arctic hares are abundant, the gyrfalcons will switch to a summer diet of mammals. Hares are eaten early in the season until the snow melts and the smaller mammals become visible to the falcons. In autumn, some gyrfalcons fly to southern regions to find food and avoid the deep winter freeze. From Greenland, some fly east over the frozen ocean to feed on eiders that are living in small polynyas, stretches of open water in the North Atlantic Ocean.

Peregrine Falcon

This falcon is one of only a few species that occur around the world. Yet, between the 1940s–1960s its populations were decimated especially in North America and Europe. DDT, a very effective and stable insecticide, used everywhere, accumulated in the falcon's food chain. DDT disrupted the deposition of calcium in eggs forming in the female's body. With thin shells, the eggs were easily crushed by the incubating adults resulting in no young falcons. The populations steadily declined until the cause was documented and DDT was banned in most of the world. Captive breeding programs in Canada, the U.S. and Europe produced young falcons that were released into the wild, re-establishing the peregrine over most of its historic range. The falcon showed its adaptability by moving into cities, living on ledges of tall buildings, which were treated as just bigger cliffs by the falcons.

Immature golden eagle (*Aquila chrysaetos*). During spring and fall more than 4,000 eagles have been counted migrating through the Canadian Rockies. To save energy, the eagles fly along mountain ridges using the uplift of crosswinds to soar and sail along the sloping sides of ridges. Alberta, Canada.

Golden Eagle

Golden eagles are supreme hunters of wild mountainous regions. Cliff and tree nesters, their stick and branch nests are used for decades, maybe for centuries until the tree dies and falls, or until the nest is destroyed by storms. Most of their food is mammals, such as rabbits and hares but they will take bigger prey, like deer and antelope. They have been known to hunt mountain sheep by knocking them off high cliffs. The eagle then feasts at its leisure on the carcass. They will also ride on the backs of antelope, attempting to sever the spinal cord with their talons. Eagles will eat carrion such as dead animals along roadsides and remnants of hunters' harvests of large mammals. A unique hunting technique has been observed in golden eagles. A pair of eagles will hunt together, with one in the lead flushing the prey, that the second eagle then attacks and kills. Together they are more successful than if they hunted individually.

Golden eagles from the Arctic and subarctic migrate south for winter. Many places in Canada, the U.S. and Europe have migration watch sites where eagles and other hawks are counted as they fly south in autumn and back north in spring. These counts are used to monitor the health of these raptor populations, most of which today appear to be healthy. Golden eagles nest in the north away from human threats. On migration and in winter, eagles face many hazards. Lead fragments from hunter bullets left in the carcass can poison the unwary eagle. Electrical poles look like easy perches to rest and watch for prey, but if the wires are not insulated, the eagle's enormous wingspan can cause a short-circuit that kills the bird. Newer threats are wind turbines along migration routes that can break a wing or otherwise fatally injure an unsuspecting bird.

Mature golden eagle. The golden eagle is a magnificent sight, symbolizing wild places. It is the best known raptor in the Northern Hemisphere. In Eurasia the golden eagle occurs along the edge of the tundra and taiga. In North America and Scandinavia the eagle is a mountain dwelling bird. Jämtland, Sweden.

Bald eagle (*Haliaeetus leucocephalus*). Eagles live near water, especially the Pacific Ocean in Western North America, reaching record densities on the west coast of British Columbia and Alaska. In Haines, Alaska, 3,000 to 4,000 eagles gather at the Bald Eagle Preserve in early fall and winter, feeding on the late run of dog salmon. Chilkat River, Alaska, USA.

Bald Eagle

The bald eagle is magnificent with a dramatic white head and tail in adult plumage. A young eagle must wait four to five years before shedding its brown head and tail. While the eagle can catch fish at the water surface, its large size enables it to steal prey from the smaller, more efficient osprey. When an osprey takes a fish, it must keep a sharp eye out for any nearby eagles that might swoop at it, an intimidating move that will cause the osprey to drop its fish. The eagle will then swoop and snatch the fish. Pirating fish or any other food, from another hunter is called kleptoparasitism.

Bald eagles live near water, especially oceans in North America, reaching highest densities on the west coast of British Columbia, Canada and Alaska. The eagles are attracted by fish and abundant marine life along the Pacific Coast. Salmon provide fertilizer to river valley plants and bald eagles help deliver the fish nutrients to the valley floors. After two to six years in the ocean, salmon return to the river where they hatched and grew before swimming out to sea. Returning salmon swim against the river's current, up shallow waterfalls and through rapids, using upstream eddies around rocks to move ahead. They spawn in the shallows of quieter waters; the female salmon lay eggs in hollows in the gravel bottom created by the males who then spray sperm over the eggs to fertilize them. All the while, bald eagles are harvesting the salmon. Young eagles are not good hunters and need easy prey. The salmon are most vulnerable while they swim in shallow water, only to die after spawning. The salmon bodies are strewn along river shorelines in autumn. Eagles take the spent bodies from the water and carry them inland, where they feed in trees. Waste from salmon bodies as well as eagle excrement provide nutrients for the ground below, encouraging a lush vegetation.

The infamous pesticide DDT used in the 1950s decimated bald eagle numbers. Fortunately, with the banning of DDT, the eagles have slowly increased into abundance. Bald eagles are again found across most of North America. Spectacular concentrations of bald eagles occur along salmon streams on the Pacific coast. Inland during winter, bald eagles concentrate in parts of California and Oregon where waterfowl prey is abundant.

The bald eagle has a high pitched call. In the 1950s, the infamous pesticide DDT decimated bald eagles. Banning of DDT has allowed eagles to slowly increase in numbers. Chilkat River, Alaska, USA.

Steller's sea eagle (*Haliaeetus pelagicus*). This huge eagle's range in Russia is now restricted to the coast of Siberia and the Kamchatka Peninsula. They have long been extinct from North America. With a wingspan of 250 cm, the raptor is the largest of all eagles. Females can weigh 9 kg and males 6 kg. Japan.

Steller's Sea Eagle

This huge eagle has a restricted range on the northeast shores of the Pacific Ocean of Siberia. In winter, juveniles move south as far as northern Japan, while adults are more likely to remain in their breeding territory. Its dramatic plumage makes it easy to identify. Its bill is longer than that of the bald eagle, and is more laterally flattened presumably to allow it to better see the end of its bill as it feeds or preens. As its name implies, this eagle is associated with fish along shorelines. It also eats a wide variety of prey from ptarmigan and capercaillie to ducks, hares, young seals and even foxes. Like other sea eagles, its large nests are located in deciduous trees, often close to shorelines. In northern Japan both species of sea eagles will take flight as fisherman head off on snowmobiles to check their nets. When a fish is tossed onto the ice the eagles try to get it often in a tug-of-war with other eagles and the fishermen. The aborigines of Hokkaido refer to this species as the "God of Eagles."

White-tailed Eagle

This widespread sea eagle occurs from Greenland across northern Siberia to Japan mostly staying in coastal areas or near large lakes and rivers. The large bill is used to eat fish, but they will also consume rabbits, ground squirrels and marmots. This species was a victim of the DDT era, suffering thin eggshells and reproductive failure. In northern Scotland, their eggs also fell victim to egg collectors and shooting by gamekeepers. Fewer than 30% of pairs produced young in the 1960s and 1970s, but after that success rates increased to over 50%. Thankfully, DDT use and egg collecting have ended and the populations have rebounded after reintroductions in some regions. These eagles weigh 3–4 kg, have a 2 m wingspan and are long-lived. Four different females and four males occupied one nest in Sweden. Over a 40 year span, one large female produced 27 young in 25 years, with three males.

White-tailed eagle (*Haliaeetus albicilla*). Small populations of this sea eagle occur in Greenland and Iceland. It is more common in Scandinavia ranging across northern Russia to the Pacific Ocean, but does not exist in North America. Lauvsnes archipelago, Norway.

Atlantic puffin (*Fratercula arctica*). The female puffin lays a single egg in a burrow that can be up to 1 m long. Puffins nest in dense colonies on coastal islands in the North Atlantic Ocean. Newfoundland, Canada.

CHAPTER NINE

Cliff Dwellers of the Arctic Ocean

Puffins

The common or Atlantic puffin nests in dense colonies on coastal islands in the North Atlantic. They nest in burrows they dig in the soil at the top of cliffs. Cliff ledges are the optimal habitat for both hatching rate and fledgling success. Competition amongst males is intense and violent, with heavier males tending to dominate. Burrow density is highest on the slopes close to the edge of the cliff. Once the ownership of those burrows is decided, fights focus on burrows on more levelled ground away from the edge. The adult puffins feed their young small fish like sand eels, herring, rocklings and sprats.

The young in the slope burrows get more food than those in level nests. This is due to the puffin's flying ability, the landing and takeoff differences on sloped versus level land. Puffins have relatively small wings which result in higher flight speed but less manoeuvrability. The birds consequently prefer nesting on slopes where they can take off and land faster and avoid gull predation. On steep slopes puffins can fly directly into their burrows, whereas on flatter land they must land and walk into the nest leaving them exposed to predatory gulls. Flatland puffin chicks receive less food causing them to emerge prematurely at the entrance to their burrows where the gulls are able to catch and eat them.

Despite losses to gulls and other predators, puffins are numerous. Twenty million Atlantic puffins roam the North

Following two pages: Horned puffin (*Fratercula corniculata*) and tufted puffin (*Fratercula cirrhata*). These two puffin species nest only in the North Pacific Ocean. Pribilof Islands, Alaska, USA.

Atlantic puffin. A puffin returns with a catch of small sand eels (*Ammodytes tobianus*). Wales, England.

Atlantic Ocean; one million horned puffins nest among rocks and cracks in cliffs in the North Pacific and three million tufted puffins feed on fish and squid also in the North Pacific. All three species have small wings that flap at 300–600 beats per minute in sustained flight and as high as 760 beats per minute at takeoff. The small wings are used to fly underwater when chasing food. Their three-toed feet are webbed for swimming and are used to manoeuvre in flight as they have very short tails.

Least auklet (*Aethia pusilla*). It is the smallest of auklets, almost the size of the snow bunting, a small songbird. The auklet is the world's most numerous seabird. Populations in Alaska have been estimated to reach 20 million birds. Pribilof Islands, Alaska, USA.

Parakeet Auklet and Least Auklet

When auklets return to nest on remote islands in the North Pacific Ocean, the nesting slopes are still covered in snow. The auklets cannot lay eggs until the snow has melted from crevices in the rocky slopes. While they wait, they court and form pairs, often with the same mate from previous years. Delays in the melting snow can drastically affect the productivity of the colonies, with late snowmelt resulting in fewer fledglings. In the Aleutian Islands, Alaska, three species of auklet occur in the same areas — least, crested and parakeet. Although they are similar in size and forage at the same time, they differ as to food resource and foraging areas. All auklets forage underwater, diving down nearly 50 m using their wings for submerged flying. Where tidal currents push water between islands, crested auklets forage on the upwelling side, whereas least auklets forage on the downstream side and parakeet auklets forage on fish and invertebrates over the top of the pass. All three species eat more when the tide is faster. As the diets of the three species are different and taken from different places, it reduces competition amongst the species for food.

Left: Parakeet auklet (*Aethia psittacula*). All species of auklets forage for food underwater, diving 50 m down and using the wings to fly underwater. Pribilof Islands, Alaska, USA.

Crested Auklet

The most obvious characteristic of this species in the breeding season is the head ornament that gives the bird its name. The curved, elongated feathers are important in the selection of mates. Dominant individuals have longer ornamental feathers. Experiments with models demonstrated that male auklets were less aggressive to models with longer feathers and attempted to dominate models with short feathers. Auklets of both sexes courted models of the opposite sex with longer feathers. Clearly the size of the crested ornament is a reflection of the condition of the auklet in the breeding season. The species has an unusually strong citrus smell. Birds with stronger odour are preferred by other auklets. The function of the odour is unknown, but it might repel ectoparasites from this very social bird that breeds in dense colonies.

Crested auklet (*Aethia cristatella*). The curved, elongated feathers are important in the selection of a mate by both sexes. Dominant individuals have longer ornamental feathers. Both sexes also have an unusually strong citrus smell, which makes them more attractive to potential mates. Pribilof Islands, Alaska, USA.

Whiskered Auklet

Whiskered auklet is another seabird that has unusual ornamental feathers.
Three white facial plumes and a long black forehead crest over the bright red bill. The whiskered auklet breeds on the remote Aleutian Islands of Alaska in the North Pacific Ocean. Their nests are scattered in rock crevices on talus slopes, cliffs and rocky beaches. Their ability to nest in such a diversity of terrain allows them to occupy more islands than other auklets. They also avoid revealing nest sites by leaving them to fish only at night. Nocturnal foraging reduces the rate at which they can deliver food, which in turn slows growth rate of their chicks. Slow growth is the price of lower predation.

Whiskered auklet (*Aethia pygmaea*). While other species of seabirds nest in large colonies, this species prefers solitary nesting sites. They are only active at night, flying to and from the ocean in the dark to attend their single egg or young and avoid predators. Iony Island, East Russia.

Common Murre

Murres are the northern hemisphere's penguins and are poor flyers. Common murres are seabirds that return to land when the urge to breed in spring overcomes their fear of land predators. They nest on broad flat ledges on cliffs or remote rocky islands. The more experienced murres nest in the middle of colonies while first-time breeders nest on the edges. They lay their single eggs on the bare rock. For some unknown reason, young that are still too small to survive sometimes head to the shoreline; adults will form a blockade to keep them away from the cold ocean until they have a full layer of waterproof feathers. Eventually the young do take the plunge into water even if they are not yet able to fly. They will remain at sea for two years before joining breeding colonies to raise their own young. In spring they gather on the sea adjacent to the breeding terrain, putting on communal displays, forming pairs and synchronizing their breeding cycles before going to the colony to lay eggs.

Above: Common murre egg. Murre lay a single egg on bare, steep rock cliffs. The egg is pear-shaped so that if disturbed, it rolls around in a circle, preventing it from falling off a narrow cliff ledge. Lofoten, Norway.

Left: Common murre (*Uria aalge*). Some individuals in the North Atlantic, known as "bridled guillemots," have a white ring around the eye.

Razorbill (*Alca torda*). The distinctive white line on the bill of the razorbill identifies it from other species. Some individuals have two white lines on their bill, a characteristic they share with the extinct great auk (*Pinguinus impennis*). Shiant Isles, Outer Hebrides, Scotland.

Razorbill

The distinctive white line on the bill distinguishes this auk from other species. Some individuals have two white lines on their bill, a characteristic they share with the extinct great auk, their closest relative. Razorbills feed on schooling fish such as capelin, herring and sand lance at ocean depths greater than 100 meters. Razorbills are long-lived seabirds that do not breed until they are four to five years old. Although each pair produces only one egg, with only 40% chance of survival, a population can grow at 6% per year in areas with 90% adult survival. However, colonies decline where adult survival is lowered by mammal predators and human harvest. Population decline also happens if chick survival falls below 40% due to worsening food supplies.

Thick-billed Murre

Like the common murre, the thick-billed murre is a poor flier and an even worse walker. This species nests on narrow ledges on high cliffs. Their relatively small wings, with high wing loading, require very fast beats to fly. However, that also means that common murres have a tough time landing on small cliff ledges especially in high winds. Sometimes they try several times before successfully putting their feet securely on the nest ledge. They like ledges high on cliffs. When they take off they simply dive off the cliff, gaining airspeed to get airborne.

The two species of murre occur in the northern oceans with common murres breeding further south and thick-billed murres breeding in the Arctic. However, they overlap a great deal and both can be found in the same nesting colonies. The nests are dense, as many as ten per square meter. Some colonies exceed one million birds. Their nutrient rich eggs are still harvested in Great Britain, Russia and some European countries. Despite this harvesting, these murres appear as abundant as they were historically. Murres are fairly heavy birds, about 1 kg, and are highly specialized for catching small fish by flying underwater. In summer the supply of small fish seems inexhaustible. The excrement of murres is rich in potash and other nutrients and fertilizes surrounding seas, adding to their biological diversity.

Thick-billed murre (*Uria lomvia*). Like the common murre, the thickbilled murre is a poor flier and an even worse walker. The murres like ledges high on cliffs. When they take off they simply dive off the cliff gaining airspeed to get airborne. Pribilof Islands, Alaska, USA.

Thick-billed murre. Two species of murre occur in the northern oceans with common murres breeding further south, whereas thick-billed murres are more common in the Arctic. However, they do overlap a great deal and both can be found in the same nesting colonies. Svalbard, Norway.

Pigeon guillemot (*Cepphus columba*). Breeds along the western coast of North America from California to Alaska's Aleutian Islands, the Bering Sea, Russia, and Japan. Monterey Bay, USA.

Black guillemot (*Cepphus grylle*). A circumpolar bird of the Arctic Oceans, it breeds on the world's arctic islands and adjacent mainland. Iceland.

Red-faced Cormorant

Even though the red-faced cormorant is a relatively large bird, it is not immune to the risks of nest predators. In Alaska, glaucous-winged gulls will harass nesting cormorants by swooping down low over them. If this intimidates a cormorant enough to drive it off its nest even a short distance, the aggressive gull will snatch an egg or young, which may be consumed on site or fed to the gull's own chicks. Marine food webs are highly complex as illustrated by predatory gulls. They eat more seabird eggs and young when sea otters are abundant near the colony. Sea otters compete with gulls for sea urchins. When otters reduce urchin density in the intertidal zone, hungry gulls are forced to seek other prey such as seabird eggs and young.

Left: Red-faced cormorant (*Phalacrocorax urile*). A rare bird about which relatively little is known. The cormorant nests along the Aleutian Islands and Bering Sea, to the eastern tip of Hokkaido Island in Japan. Pribilof Islands, Alaska, USA.

Guillemots

Guillemots are diving seabirds that forage near shore in water as deep as 30 meters. A study of pigeon guillemot found that some pairs were specialized in their diet while others were diet generalists. The specialists caught larger open water schooling prey like sand lance and herring that are high in fats, while generalists ate smaller bottom-living fish such as sculpins and blennies, which have low fat levels. The specialist's chicks grew faster and survived better than the chicks of the generalist guillemots. However, the diets and survivals varied each year depending upon the abundance of the larger, fatter fish. These increase when water temperatures increase, possibly a benefit of climate change. The bottom-living fish varies less in annual numbers. If the larger fat-rich fish are available, more guillemots become specialists and forage on these fish, but in lean years they are forced to forage on bottom-living fish. Not only are schooling fish richer in fat, but they provide more nutrition per unit, helping adult guillemots raise two chicks instead of one, or to spend more time resting while raising just a single chick.

Dovekie or little auk (*Alle alle*). The little auk is about the size of the European starling and breeds in huge colonies on steep cliff sides. The most numerous arctic seabird, their population is estimated at 24 million, with the main concentrations on the east and west coasts of Greenland. Large colonies also occur on Russia's arctic islands, Novaya Zemlya and Severnaya Zemlya, as well as on Svalbard, Norway.

Dovekie

Dovekie is a small arctic nesting seabird that gathers in the millions. In one year, 13 million were recorded in northwest Baffin Bay, during spring migration, en route to breeding colonies in Greenland and the Canadian arctic islands. They forage in open channels on the ice where their food of zooplankton is concentrated. If warm water is pushed north, replacing cold Arctic Ocean waters, the quantity of food declines affecting the growth and survival of their young. In winter,

dovekies concentrate offshore over the Grand Banks off the Canadian East Coast, the outer slopes of the continental shelf. Like other seabirds, dovekies spend most of their year in the open ocean. While feeding, they are vulnerable to many human threats such as oil spills, entanglement in fishing nets, fatal attraction to ships lights, predators and the current warming of the Arctic Ocean.

Black-legged kittiwake (*Rissa tridactyla*). Adult Kittiwake diving for spawning sockeye salmon eggs. They also eat salmon scraps left by bears. Prince William Sound, Alaska, USA.

Black-legged kittiwake (*Rissa tridactyla*). Kittiwakes have brightly colored orange mouths, pink-orange tongues, red eye rings and yellow bills. The red comes from carotenoids in their nutritious ocean food such as shrimp. Svalbard, Norway.

Kittiwakes

Kittiwakes are one of the most abundant gull species in the Northern Hemisphere. They feed on small schooling fish such as sand lance, capelin and herring, as well as on carotenoid rich krill and small crustaceans known as copepods. They will fly up to 70 km away from their nesting colony to gather food for the nestlings. Female birds often let bright colors decide the choice of a male mate. Kittiwakes have a brightly colored orange mouth, pink-orange tongue, red eye ring, yellow bill and red-legged carmine feet. The red comes from carotenoids in the nutritious ocean foods. Males with more carotenoids in their blood have brighter colors and produce more chicks. Thus each male's success is dependent upon the abundance of carotenoid rich food before the breeding season. Just finding enough food to eat is not enough, they need to increase their color intensity in order to find a mate.

Red-legged kittiwake (*Rissa brevirostris*). The rare bird is one of the most sought after gulls by birdwatchers.
Pribilof Islands, Alaska, USA.

Whooper swan (*Cygnus cygnus*). Male on a peat bog guarding incubating female. Once a rare wilderness bird in Lappland, it is now fairly common and even breeds in southern Sweden. They nest in the Subarctic from Scandinavia across Eurasia to Russia's Kamchatka. The whooper swan is the national bird of Finland. Kuhmo, Finland.

CHAPTER TEN

Birds of the Midnight Sun

Whooper Swan

Some species of swan were named after their calls: whistling, trumpeter and whooper swans all have long winding windpipes. Whistling, now called tundra swan, has the highest pitch call, a melodious wow-how-ow laughter. The trumpeter has a straight section in its windpipe that gives it a low, deeper call. The whooper swan's call is as its name suggests, a loud whoop as it flies past. When shot, swans make a unique sound as they tumble to the ground. This may be the origin of the term "swan song."

Bewick's Swan

Bewick's swan was once considered a separate species because of its small size and the large yellow base of the bill. Currently it is considered a subspecies of the tundra swan. This Eurasian swan breeds across the Russian Arctic from the Kanin Peninsula to the Chukchi Sea, far from most human interference. From there it migrates to three general areas: Western Europe, the Caspian Sea and coastal Southeast Asia. These coastal wetlands suffer from water pollution and when they get converted to human use the swans must depend upon agricultural lands for food. In one study half the swans had lead poisoning in their bodies from ingestion of lead shots from duck hunters. They are not endangered but their numbers are in decline. Thomas Bewick, after whom this swan is named, was a friend of the American artist John James Audubon and author of *A History of British Birds*, published in the late 18th century.

Bewick's swan (*Cygnus columbianus bewickii*). This swan is now considered a subspecies of the tundra swan. Switzerland.

Tundra swan (*Cygnus columbianus*). Tundra swans nest in scattered pairs in the Arctic, safe from most human influence. Although they were hunted during migration, the harvest was sustainable. Alaska, USA.

Tundra Swan

Although they were hunted intensely by early settlers in the Americas, tundra swans were never as endangered as the trumpeter swan. Tundra swans nest in the Arctic in scattered pairs safe from most human influence. Although they were hunted while migrating, the harvest was sustainable because they were safe on their coastal wintering habitats. In the arctic summer, 24 hours of daylight warmth fosters a rich bloom of plants. Swans are herbivores, eating the nutritious vegetation during the brief season. They arrive before all the snow melts and the female uses stored energy to produce a clutch of three to five eggs. As the vegetation becomes nutritious, the cygnets hatch and feed themselves. The parents stand guard against predators and provide shelter during inclement weather.

Trumpeter Swan

Weighing 10–17 kg these swans used to nest from Alaska south across the Great Plains. Overharvest eliminated the southern breeding populations leaving the trumpeter swan on the brink of extinction. Biologists fortunately determined how to reestablish this swan in parts of its former range. Swans stay as a family group throughout their first winter, then return to the northern breeding grounds; young swans return to the location where they first learned to fly. The reintroduction technique requires capturing whole families in the northern breeding grounds when the adults are molting their wingfeathers and before the young learn to fly. Then families are released on suitable southern wetlands. In spring the adults return to their original breeding area but the young return to the new foster wetlands. Since swans do not breed until they are five years old, successful reintroductions of swans in the south have taken several decades.

Trumpeter swan (*Cygnus buccinator*). Overharvesting eliminated the southern breeding population leaving the trumpeter swan on the brink of extinction. Alaska, USA.

Tundra swans. Spring birds taking flight from a prairie pond. High flying migratory birds have been observed by pilots at altitudes well over 6,000 meters. The swans travel thousands of kilometers from arctic breeding grounds to winter quarters in California and Nevada. Alberta, Canada.

Barnacle goose (*Branta leucopsis*). Parents with goslings. Cliff dwelling geese build their nests on steep mountains, well protected from arctic foxes and polar bears. Breeding grounds are Greenland, Svalbard and Novaya Zemlya. The barnacle goose began nesting in Sweden in 1971. Svalbard, Norway.

Barnacle Goose

Barnacle geese congregate in large flocks in winter, partly because their food source is concentrated and partly to avoid predators. However, such concentration leads to competition for grasses and other plants. Flocks of geese move across grasslands with a feeding hierarchy; large families feed before small families. Levels of aggression vary with age and sex; older geese are more aggressive than young geese and males are more forward than females. The aggressive geese peck at food faster and spend more time defending the grasses and since they are at the leading edge of the flock, the food is more abundant. Subordinate geese in the middle of the flock feed on the leftovers.

Blue Goose

Blue goose is a color morph of the pure white snow goose with bluish-gray plumage replacing the white except for the head. The dark phase is caused by a single dominant gene, thus a white snow goose must have two recessive genes. Blue and snow geese interbreed freely in their arctic and subarctic breeding sites. Since they nest on the ground the eggs are easy meals for predators. If the geese nest close to snowy owls or rough-legged hawks, predators are less likely to take their eggs. Predators such as the arctic fox and jaegers are deterred from approaching the nests of large raptors. However, if a bear takes an interest in the geese nests, large raptors are no deterrent.

Snow goose (*Chen caerulescens*). Blue morph parent with gosling. The snow goose has two color phases, white and blue. They were once believed to be separate species. Hudson Bay, Canada.

Arctic fox. Fox in midspring molt, stealing a snow goose egg. Wrangel Island, Russia.

Snow goose (*Chen caerulescens*). Geese landing in Bosque del Apache National Wildlife Refuge which has recorded 377 birds species. In winter, large numbers of migratory birds can be found here including 10,000 sandhill cranes and 20,000 snow geese. New Mexico, USA.

Snow Goose

A harbinger of spring, snow geese fly north in huge flocks covering fields like snow. The species is a conservation success story that has become too successful. In the early 1900's snow geese were in decline and overharvested like many large birds in North America. The Canadian Migratory Birds Convention Act 1917 between Canada and USA (significantly updated in 1994), brought regulations to the hunt. As agriculture expanded, particularly in the Southern States, snow geese prospered by feeding on spilled grain in harvested fields. Then rice was introduced to the agriculture of the Gulf states and geese

numbers now increase by five percent annually. With over five million snow geese, their arctic breeding grounds are overgrazed causing long term damage to the tundra. The short growing seasons don't allow the tundra plants full recovery from year to year. Reduced food supply has affected body size. Goslings weight have declined more than 16% and their bones are two to four percent shorter. Consequently, the adult geese that return to breed weigh less and are smaller. They also have fewer eggs and young each year. This decline will be compounded with the effects of climate change.

Snow goose (*Chen caerulescens*). Flock taking flight from Wrangel Island, which is a fully protected wildlife and nature sanctuary located between the East Siberian Sea and Chukchi Sea, close to the Russian mainland and about 500 km west of Alaska. Besides several mammal species, the flora and fauna on the island includes 417 plant species and 65 bird species. Wrangel Island, Russia.

Mackenzie River Delta, Northwest Territories, Canada. The myriad of delta islands are important resting and breeding areas for migratory birds.

Mackenzie River Delta

The Mackenzie River is the largest and longest river in Canada, flowing 1,700 km north from Great Slave Lake through the Northwest Territories to the Arctic emptying through a huge river delta into the Beaufort Sea. The delta is an important resting and breeding area for more than 400,000 migratory birds that fly north each spring. Its islands are an important staging ground in late August through September for the million plus birds that migrate south. Snow geese are the most numerous; 323,000 were counted in 1975. However, greater white-fronted goose and tundra swan are also abundant. Over 200 bird species have been recorded in the delta.

Sandhill Crane

This tall, elegant crane nests across the boreal forest south into the United States with non migrant populations in the south. Overharvesting a century ago reduced their numbers but today about half a million cranes migrate from Canada to the USA. In winter they compete with the more abundant snow geese for grain waste in agricultural landscapes. In the late 1900's migrating young sandhill cranes were tracked from a nesting area in Ontario 900 km to wintering sites in Virginia by ultralight aircraft over a 21 day period. In the spring the cranes returned the same route back to Ontario on their own. This experiment was then used with the endangered whooping crane to establish a new population that migrates from Wisconsin to Florida.

Right: Sandhill crane (*Grus canadensis*) during fall migration.
Northwest Territories, Canada.

Eurasian crane (*Grus grus*). Adult bird on nest with one newborn chick. Normally, two eggs are laid and incubated for 29 to 31 days. Sweden.

Eurasian Crane

Eurasian crane, also known as the common crane, breeds on open bogs and wetlands in Scandinavia, northern parts of Asia and Russia. Author and zoologist Bengt Berg (1885–1967) made the Swedish crane migration famous with his 1922 book, *With Cranes to Africa*. Every year, returning from their wintering quarters in Spain and Africa, more than 20,000 cranes stop in Sweden at Lake Hornborgarsjön, which is the most famous bird lake in northern Europe. A record count of 26,000 cranes was made there April 3, 2012.

Cranes have gray feathers overall, but during the nesting season the cranes stain their feathers by preening, using their long bills to rub iron-rich oxide mud through their upper back, breast and lower neck feathers for a rusty appearance. It is believed this change in color makes them less conspicuous at the nest site. The crane is a big bird and can weigh up to 8 kg, length of 130 cm and wingspan of 240 cm. The birds bond during breeding season and live in monogamy throughout their adult life.

Right: Eurasian cranes perform mating dances and often go into duets. Sweden.

Wilson's snipe (*Gallinago delicata*). When disturbed, this bird takes off in a zigzag pattern to avoid predators. Alaska, USA.

Wilson's snipe nest with 4 eggs. Waterton Lakes National Park, Canada.

Wilson's Snipe

One sign of spring in the Northern Hemisphere is the aerial display of snipe winnowing over wetlands. The males fly in high circles, then dive steeply, creating a winnowing sound from the vibration of tail feathers. This ungainly looking shorebird has a long bill and short legs. They are adapted to skulking through grassy edges of wetlands looking for insects, earthworms and other food. When disturbed, they take off in a zigzag pattern to avoid any aerial predator nearby.

Ruff (*Philomachus pugnax*). Males on lek displaying colorful head tufts. The spectacular drama plays out in silence, except for the sound of a few wing smatters. Varanger Peninsula, Norway.

Ruff

The Ruff is a distinctive shorebird with the male's dramatic head feathering and orange facial skin. The species is named after the fashionable ladies decorative collar worn by ladies in the 17th century. The rare plumage is matched by an unusual mating procedure. Males gather in mating arenas, called leks, and the smaller females, reeves, watch the displaying males before deciding on a mate. Unfortunately, most of these displays happen in northern Eurasia, far from human admirers. Some do mate in Western Europe, where they can be observed. The males leave after mating and wander leisurely south in midsummer. Once the young can fly, they migrate with the females to Africa for the winter.

Red knot (*Calidris canutus*) on arctic breeding grounds. Red knot populations are in decline. They weight less than in the past, suggesting a decreasing food supply. Alaska, USA.

Red Knot

Wetlands are important in the life cycle for bird species. An example is Delaware Bay, on the US East Coast for three species of shorebirds: red knot, ruddy turnstone and sanderling. In May, during the shorebird's northward migration, they stop here to feed on the eggs of horseshoe crabs. The birds stay for up to a month, increasing weight by an incredible 55–70%. These fat reserves sustain their 3,000 km flight north to the Arctic, and the ensuing quick production of eggs during the short arctic summer. However, red knot populations are still in decline, due to heavy commercial harvests of horseshoe crabs. The weight gain is not as great as in the past. This could result in poor survival on their northward migration, with few birds able to breed successfully. The harvest of horseshoe crabs in Delaware Bay peaked at three million in 1997. Since then, commercial harvest has been reduced, but only time will tell if this helps the red knot population to recover.

Bar-tailed Godwit

The bar-tailed godwit holds the record for non-stop migration, over 11,000 km each way in eight days, along the north-south length of the Pacific Ocean between Alaska and New Zealand. In preparation for this epic migration, they gain fat equal to the weight of the rest of their body by eating marine invertebrates and other nutritious foods. To reduce additional weight load, they shrink their internal organs — liver, kidney, gizzard and digestive tract. They rebuild the organs at the end of the migrations, twice per year. The godwits must find favorable winds to complete the distance. Godwits in northern Europe fly to Central Africa, a distance of 4,300 km, by changing altitude, as much as up to 5.5 km to gain an average of 18 kph during their flight.

Right: Bar-tailed godwit (*Limosa lapponica*). Male calling in breeding plumage. This bird holds the record for non-stop migration. Varanger Peninsula, Norway.

Spoon-billed sandpiper (*Eurynorhynchus pygmeus*). Bird in winter plumage feeding on salt flats in southern Thailand. One of the rarest arctic birds; less than 100 pairs nest in eastern Siberia.

Spoon-billed Sandpiper

This arctic shorebird has an unusual flattened bill which it sweeps from side to side when feeding in freshwater ponds on the coasts of Eastern Siberia, the Chukchi Sea and the Kamchatka Peninsula. The sandpipers then migrate south, along the western coast of the Pacific Ocean to winter in Southeast Asia. Destruction of shoreline habitat and overhunting has reduced the breeding population to less than 100 pairs, making this species critically endangered. A captive breeding program is underway to raise young for release back into the wild.

Sanderling

Sanderlings breed in the high Arctic around the world and migrate 3,000 to 10,000 km south to warmer coastal sandy beaches for the winter. This comical shorebird can be watched chasing each wave. Sanderlings run rapidly, stopping frequently to pick up small crabs, beetles, mussels, clams, amphipods, flies and other invertebrates. The crustaceans live deep in the sand but come to the surface at high tide to feed on plankton and detritus washed in with the waves. The sanderlings probe the sand randomly, grabbing any prey they touch by chance. In Delaware Bay, they eat horseshoe crab eggs, but unlike other species of shorebirds, sanderlings have a varied diet that gives them some protection from food shortages.

Sanderling (*Calidris alba*). During migration sanderlings are found on warm sandy beaches around the world. They run rapidly, stopping frequently to pick up small food items. Galapagos Islands.

Ruddy turnstone (*Arenaria interpres*). Turnstones in breeding plumage. This bird got its name from its habit of turning over small stones looking for molluscs and insects. Terschelling, Holland.

Ruddy Turnstone

This colorful shorebird leaves its arctic breeding grounds and spends most of its migration and winter seasons on rocky shores. Turnstones that winter in Australia spend their summer in eastern Siberia and Alaska. Some non-stop flights of 7,600 km take six days of continuous travel. At stopovers the turnstones forage busily to store fat before the next long flight. In a year, the turnstones travel about 27,000 km, much of it over the open Pacific Ocean. The bird got its name from its habit of turning over small stones, looking for molluscs and insects.

Grey or Red Phalarope

With two quite different names, one wonders if bird watchers are color blind. However, this bird is known as red phalarope in North America, where it breeds in the high Arctic and the female has a bright red color. In Europe where most sightings are of wintering phalaropes, they are a dull gray. Like other phalaropes, the females are more brightly colored than the males. After courtship, the females lay four eggs and then leave the better camouflaged male to incubate and care for the young. After rearing the young in arctic environments, both sexes mix on the open ocean, where they feed. The distance between breeding and wintering areas can be amazing. One phalarope of a similar species, the red-necked phalarope, migrated west from northern Scotland to North America, south down the east coast to Mexico and across the Caribbean and Central America to the Pacific Ocean to winter off the coast of Peru, a one-way journey of 8,000 km.

Right: Grey phalarope (*Phalaropus fulicarius*). After courtship and mating the female lays four eggs, then leaves the better camouflaged male to incubate and care for the young. Iceland.

Whimbrel (*Numenius phaeopus*). Fighting with a crab on an African mudflat. It feeds on fiddler crabs by probing their burrows with the long beak. A world traveller, one whimbrel, tracked by satellite transmitter, flew 5,100 km in five days to land on Bahamian island. Gambia, Africa.

Black-bellied plover (*Pluvialis squatarola*). Male in breeding plumage sounding alarm call. It breeds from Russia's Kanin Peninsula across Arctic Siberia to Alaska and Canada's arctic islands. One of the largest plovers, it feeds on fiddler crabs. Seward Peninsula, Alaska, USA.

Whimbrel

Arctic nesting whimbrel head south during the peak of the Atlantic hurricane season. One whimbrel, tracked by a satellite transmitter, flew 5,100 km in five days before encountering Hurricane Irene. Even though it flew into the eye of the hurricane, it was persistent and landed on a Bahamian island. Another whimbrel flew into a tropical storm off the coast of Nova Scotia; for 27 hours she only averaged a ground speed of 14 kph before finally reaching a tailwind and headed to land at 147 kph. Whimbrel breeding in Alaska and wintering in the Caribbean and South America, travel about 25,000 km per year. Other Alaska whimbrels avoid hurricanes by travelling a shorter route along the Pacific coast to Central America.

Black-bellied Plover

This arctic breeder has a relatively short bill for a shorebird. Although its diet is varied with fly larvae and invertebrates from sandy beaches, its specialty is fiddler crabs, caught with the strong bill. If a plover approaches a fiddler crab and fails to catch it, the fortunate crab will retreat into its sandy hole. A predator-prey game of patience then ensues. The plover has to decide whether to wait for the crab to emerge, or go elsewhere. The crab needs to come out to feed. Apparently in most situations, the crab is more patient and the unlucky plover decides to try its luck on another crab.

Bluethroat (*Luscinia svecica*). Male singing near the Arctic Circle. Inari, Finland.

Northern wheatear (*Oenanthe oenanthe*) male. Breeds on Baffin Island, Canada, and migrates across the northern Atlantic to Great Britain; from there they continue migrating to Mauritania, West Africa. Shetland Islands, Scotland.

Bluethroat

Bluethroats are typical territorial songbirds that nest in wetland shrubbery across northern Europe and Asia, with a few in Alaska. Although these birds appear monogamous, one third of bluethroat nests contain at least one young that was fathered by a second male. Overall, one-fifth of young bluethroats are fathered by a different male than the one that feeds them. The mixed broods are random and occur in clusters. Apparently, certain broods have half the young from a second male. Studies of males show that if they spend up to 60% of their time guarding their females, they are less likely to have young from another male in the nest.

Northern Wheatear

Weighing only 25 grams, this tiny arctic passerine flies long distances. A small population breeds on Baffin Island in Canada's Eastern Arctic, but they are not seen further south. Instead, they fly across the northern Atlantic to Great Britain and then winter in Mauritania in West Africa, a round trip of 15,000 km. The Alaska population travels even further. They head west across the Bering Sea, through Siberia and the Middle East to Sudan and Uganda in East Africa. Wheatears breed across the Arctic and the Old World, then winter across Central Africa, with a few making it as far as South Africa in summer.

White Wagtail

White wagtail (*Motacilla alba*). In Western Europe they are called pied wagtail due to the more extensive dark feathering; elsewhere they are whiter. Ask, Skåne, Sweden.

As their name suggests, wagtails wag their tales. No one has yet suggested a convincing reason for the action. Wagtails inhabit short vegetation where they feed on insects. They breed in northern regions of Eurasia and migrate into the tropics of Africa and Asia for the winter. In milder climates some wagtails stay year-round. Wagtails exploit a wide range of open habitats created by humans, even parking lots of shopping malls. White wagtails are whiter, but still have variable patterns. Those patterns are darkest in Western Europe where they are called pied wagtail.

Horned Lark

Horned lark (*Eremophila alpestris*). This lark is one of the most successful songbirds. It nests from grassland prairie to arctic tundra. Only one lark species is found in North America. Mittåkläppen, Härjedalen, Sweden.

Horned lark is one of the most successful songbirds, nesting from grassland prairie to arctic tundra. Isolated populations occur in the mountains of Columbia in South America and in the Atlas Mountains of Morocco, Africa. Their success is even more surprising, since they nest on the ground in an open cup nest easily accessible to predators. While the males are so visible with their aerial soaring and song, the females and nests are obscure. The nests can be in ploughed fields in the south or barren gravel ridges in the Arctic, places that melt early and are almost free of vegetation. Both adults feed the young and do so rapidly, barely stopping in what appears to be continuous small movements while catching insects. A watching predator would not be led to the nest easily.

Snow bunting (*Plectrophenax nivalis*). Singing male in breeding plumage. The most northerly recorded passerine was seen by observers in an American submarine at the North Pole. Iceland.

Lapland longspur (*Calcarius lapponicus*). Singing male in breeding plumage. A circumpolar bird that breeds north of the treeline from Alaska east to Kamchatka. One of the most abundant arctic birds. Alaska, USA.

Snow Bunting and Lapland Longspur

These two hardy songbirds arrive on the arctic tundra and begin to nest as the first patches of bare ground appear. However, they live different lives. The bunting is 30% larger and nests in rock cavities; the smaller longspur lays eggs in an open cup nest in the arctic vegetation. Open nests are more vulnerable to predators, so the longspur must raise its young quickly in seven days. The more protected rock cavities allow the bunting to take more time, 13 days. All songbird young rely on the adults for food and warmth, typically provided by the female, while the male does more foraging. The adults take advantage of the 24-hour daylight by searching for food, mostly insects, for up to 22 hours per day. The longspur young manage to keep warm on their own by the seventh day, and then leave the nest, presumably to avoid predators, while the more secure bunting young stay in the protective rock nest for about five more days. Nesting in the short arctic summer has to be efficient as darkness and cold will soon arrive and both species must head south to temperate latitudes for the winter.

Female common redpoll. For most of the 20th century the number of wintering redpolls in Canada was high on odd numbered years and low on even numbered years. Alberta, Canada.

Common Redpoll

Another hardy subarctic songbird, redpolls breed around the high latitudes of the world and move to mid latitudes in winter. They nest year round in shrubs up to 3 m from the ground. They often feed beneath taller shrubs such as alder and birch in winter, when these can protect thinner snow under them, gives redpolls access to seeds that would otherwise be covered. When redpoll forage on seeds of roadside plants during winter, they risk being killed by vehicles. For most of the 20th century, the number of wintering redpolls in Canada was high on odd-numbered years and low on even-numbered years. Since about 2005, this biannual pattern has started to fail with more years between "highs." The causes are unclear.

Pine Grosbeak

This large finch breeds in coniferous forest around the Northern Hemisphere. One of their main foods is spruce seeds, and their reproductive rate varies with the supply of seeds. In years when spruce have bumper crops of cones and seeds, grosbeaks and other boreal finches also have bumper broads of young. Squirrels, chipmunks and even mice prosper in those years. In the following winter, grosbeaks often arrive at bird feeders in the south in large numbers.

Left: Pine grosbeak (*Pinicola enucleator*). Their reproductive rate is governed by the supply of spruce seeds. Alberta, Canada.

Male common redpoll (*Carduelis flammea*). Alberta, Canada.

Siberian tit (*Poecile cinctus*). Known in North America as gray-headed chickadee. The tit ranges from northern Scandinavia across Siberia, but is rare in Alaska and northwest Yukon, Canada. It is a hardy bird that can survive temperatures as low as -60°C. Finland.

Siberian Jay

Another cold hardy songbird of the northern forests, this and other jay species store food in the autumn for winter and spring use when food is scarce. They wrap insects and other food in saliva from their large saliva glands and store it on dead branches that are usually not visited by other foraging birds. They make hundreds of such storage sites. Although one young Siberian jay from a brood will typically remain with its parents through the winter, the parents rarely share their food caches, retrieving them mostly for themselves. The jay nests in late winter, while snow is on the ground. The nest is about 5 cm thick to insulate the eggs and the incubating female from the cold.

Left: Siberian jay (*Perisoreus infaustus*). Jämtland, The jay nests from the middle of March through April, while snow is still on the ground. Jämtland, Sweden.

Siberian Tit

As its name implies, this tit or chickadee occurs across cold Siberia west to Scandinavia and east to Alaska and adjacent Canada. To survive the cold winter nights, these small birds use a few special strategies. They seek shelter either in a tree cavity or burrow into the snow. Tree cavities have the best energy-saving benefit when an old nest provides added insulation. Tits can drop their body temperatures down to 7°C below their daytime temperature of about 42°C, a controlled state of hypothermia. They reduce their metabolic rate up to 50% and will roost together, further conserving energy on cold nights. These adaptations allow them to survive the cold northern winters.

Red-throated loon (*Gavia stellata*). Incubating adult. This loon is the smallest of its family and nests on small arctic ponds. Victoria Island, Nunavut, Canada.

CHAPTER ELEVEN

Birds of the Polar Seas

Loons

The five loon species are all divers that specialize in catching fish underwater. Their legs are far back on their bodies, positioned like a diver's flippers, which is optimal for swimming underwater. When the loons take off to fly they cannot launch directly off the water surface; their chest muscles aren't large enough and their legs are too far back. They must run across the surface to gain enough airspeed to achieve lift. A cumbersome approach to flight but the body is made for diving for food.

Red-throated Loon

In North America this family of waterbirds is called loons; in Europe the name is divers. The red-throated loon is the smallest and, not surprisingly, nests on smaller shallower arctic ponds. Breeding adults form long term pair bonds, returning to the same pond each summer. Even though these loons are attentive to their nest of eggs and chicks and have a camouflage patterned back, the nests in shallow waters are vulnerable to predators such as gulls, jaegers and foxes. The oldest known red-throated loon lived 23 years and seven months before it was found dead, covered in oil on a beach in Sweden.

Red-throated loon. Male displaying its distinctive red-colored throat. Finland.

Pacific loon (*Gavia pacifica*). Young are born dark brown but later change to a lighter brownish downy plumage. Alaska, USA.

Pacific and Arctic Loons

These loons occur around the globe in the Northern Hemisphere. The arctic loon, an Old World species is rare in North America and nests there only on the Seward Peninsula, Alaska. In recent decades it has increased in numbers in the United Kingdom thanks to the installation of artificial nesting rafts in northern lochs. Unfortunately, they are declining elsewhere in Europe due to shrinking stocks of fish which are their prey. The decrease in fish is caused by warming of the North Sea where the loons winter. The similar Pacific loon has a circumpolar spread from Scandinavia across Siberia to northern Canada and as far east as Baffin Island. They winter along the Pacific coast as far south as California. Loons lose all their feathers at the same time in late winter, then have to regrow them before flying north again. On migration they stop at ocean upwellings where zoo plankton and predatory fish are more abundant. After refuelling, the loons continue but avoid flying into headwinds and wait until south winds blow, which helps them to fly north back to the breeding grounds.

Arctic loon (*Gavia arctica*). They range across northern Europe and Russia. A small population breeds on Alaska's Seward Peninsula.Kotjärnet, Värmland, Sweden.

Common loon (*Gavia Immer*) with young. At up to 8 kg this heavy bird cannot get airborn without using its large webbed feet to run across the surface of the water, preferably into a strong headwind. Lake Myvatn, Iceland.

Common loon. Nest normally contains two eggs, but sometimes one or three. British Columbia, Canada.

Common Loon

This species of loon occurs across North America, Greenland, Iceland and Great Britain. Its calls are global symbols of wilderness. Each call has specific meaning to other loons. The yodel is given only by males to establish territories and to challenge other males that trespass on the same lake or fly over. The tremolo or laughing call signals alarm or distress caused by threats or territorial disputes. The tremolo is the only call they make in flight, or on the water, to call to a loon flying overhead. The wail with up to three notes is given to let distant family members know where they are. The hoot is a soft intimate call to let closer family groups or small flocks know their whereabouts and to summon young for food. Variations within these categories may provide additional information to fellow loons, but humans have yet to interpret them.

Yellow-billed loon (*Gavia adamsii*). Adult in breeding plumage. There are five species of loons and the yellow-billed loon is the rarest. It nests in Russia, Alaska and Canada. Siberia, Russia.

Yellow-billed Loon

The rarest of the family, the yellow-billed loon is also the largest. It nests almost exclusively north of the Arctic Circle, and primarily in freshwater tundra ponds. It winters on the east and west shores of the Pacific Ocean at mid-latitudes.

During summer, south of its breeding range, the loon is often seen on Great Bear Lake and Great Slave Lake in the Northwest Territories, Canada. Its large yellow bill easily distinguishes it from the more common loon.

King eider (*Somateria spectabilis*). Drake lifting from a shore lead. The bird's common name, king eider, is a direct translation of its Icelandic name, "king" for its orange crownlike knob. Victoria Island, Nunavut, Canada.

Common eider (*Somateria mollissima*). Adult drake. In Norway on Vega Island, eiderdown is collected commercially at eider farms, which preserve old harvest traditions and are protected as World Heritage Sites. The eiders nest in strategically placed wood houses or nesting boxes. Träslövläge, Sweden.

King Eider

Detailed studies of king eider migrations show this species has flexible patterns of movement that might make it better able to respond to climate changes. Eiders nest in northwest Canada and northern Alaska. Males do not help to raise young eiders, so males leave the breeding areas first from mid June to late July, about a month before females migrate. They fly along the coast of the Beaufort Sea to the west side of the Bering Sea where they molt their feathers. The males travel only 80 km per day compared to the females who catch up by traveling 120 km per day. This migration is over 3,000 km long for the Canadian eiders. The molt takes up to three months before they disperse to ocean winter homes in the northern Pacific Ocean from southwestern Alaska across the islands to eastern Siberia. In March they fly along the coasts up to 6,000 km back to their breeding grounds.

Common Eider

Eiderdown, the warm feathers of sleeping bags, duvets and coats is associated with common eiders that breed across the arctic coast of Europe, North America and eastern Siberia. This sea duck lives on the ocean but comes to fresh water lakes to nest. It dives for marine prey including mussels and crabs. Mussels are eaten whole and crushed in the eider gizzard and the shells are excreted; crabs are declawed then eaten whole. Eiders winter on the ocean where warm water upwellings stay icefree. In Hudson Bay the ice circulation keeps open water on the downstream side of the Belcher Islands where eiders winter in large numbers. The local Sanikiluaq community is known as the "People of the Feather", since they derive food and clothing by harvesting eiders. This ecosystem is under threat because of the release of fresh water in winter from Quebec hydro dams which produce electricity for New England. The fresh water overlies seawater and freezes, restricting the areas where eiders can feed causing large population declines.

Steller's eider (*Polysticta stelleri*). Adult drakes. German physician Georg Wilhelm Steller discovered the bird in 1751 when he sailed with Vitus Bering's Russian expedition. Alaska, USA.

Steller's Eider

This is the smallest and fastest flying eider. It breeds in freshwater tundra ponds from Russia's Tajmyr Peninsula through the Chukchi and Bering seas to the northern slope of Alaska's west coast. The German physician, Georg Wilhelm Steller, discovered the bird in 1751 when he sailed with the Russian Vitus Bering's expedition. Steller's Eider was known in Sweden as "Alförrädare," meaning "betraying." The name originated around 1820 by local fishermen on the Baltic east coast in Södermanlands archipelago. When this eider was first seen in spring the bird revealed that "Alfågeln" the long-tailed duck should soon arrive and it was time to erect nets over the water to catch the fast flying small 1 kg ducks — an important food for early Swedish households.

Spectacled Eider

This rarely seen eider is dispersed across the coastal lowlands of Siberia and Alaska during summer, then congregates during winter in ice free areas of the Pacific just south of Bering Strait. The USA has classified it as "threatened" under its Endangered Species Act, due to severe declines in Western Alaska. They are superbly adapted to life on the open sea where the males spend 11 months of the year, returning to shore only to breed. They even molt at sea, two to 45 km from shore. They dive for clams on the ocean floor. The young leave the breeding grounds with the females remaining at sea for two to three years before the first breeding.

Spectacled eider (*Somateria fischeri*). Adult drake. The USA has classified this bird as "threatened" under its Endangered Species Act due to its severe decline in Western Alaska, USA.

Red-breasted merganser (*Mergus serrator*). Female leading her four full-grown offspring. This circumpolar merganser nests on the ground from the northern boreal forest up to the arctic coast in habitats with fresh water lakes and streams. Lake Clark National Park, Alaska.

Red-breasted merganser (*Mergus serrator*). Male showing straggly greenish crest in a courtship display.
Prince Albert National Park, Canada.

Common merganser (*Mergus merganser*). In Europe this bird is also known as Goosander. Switzerland.

Red-breasted and Common Merganser

Mergansers are large diving ducks that feed primarily on fish. The red-breasted nests on the ground further north and winters in salt water on both coasts of North America. Within a day of hatching the young are led to water where they feed themselves. Unable to dive, the young feed on insects in shallow water. Several broods may group with one or more females in attendance, but not to feed them. The advantage of several broods together is to reduce the risk of predation for

any individual young. The common merganser, also known as fishduck or sawbill, nests across the boreal forests of North America and at similar latitudes across Europe. The birds nest in large tree cavities where the female lays eight to 11 eggs. The young must jump from the high nest site before the female leads them to water to feed for themselves. The young must survive 65–70 days before they can fly.

Barrow's goldeneye (*Bucephala islandica*). Male marked with leg band. Breeds mainly in western Canada and Alaska. It is a common nester in Iceland at Lake Myvatn, which is surrounded by rich wetlands. Rare vagrant to Europe and Scandinavia. Barrier Lake, Rocky Mountains, Canada.

Barrow's and Common Goldeneye

Common goldeneye are widespread across North America and Eurasia to Siberia. Barrow's goldeneye has a restricted breeding range in western North America and a disjointed range in Iceland. These diving ducks are unusual as they stay paired year after year. Other ducks have different mates each breeding season. Goldeneye females frequently return to the same breeding territory and even the same nest. Their mates join them both in summer and frequently later in winter habitat even though they are separated during molt. Whereas most duck species nest on the ground, goldeneye are among the few ducks that nest in tree cavities. Most cavities are produced by large woodpeckers, pileated in North America and black in Eurasia. The availability of nest sites depends upon the abundance of the woodpeckers. Both goldeneye species will use artificial nest boxes, a positive conservation measure the public can easily take part in. Boxes should be near wetlands where the goldeneyes feed on aquatic invertebrates, including crustaceans and molluscs.

Common goldeneye (*Bucephala clangula*). Male during takeoff. Goldeneye nest in tree cavities but will readily use artificial nest boxes. Getterön, Sweden.

Long-tailed duck (*Clangula hyemalis*). Male in winter plumage. This duck is a circumpolar breeder on the arctic coast. One of the most important wintering areas is the Baltic Sea where about four to five million gather. The world population is estimated at eight million. Prince William Sound, Alaska, USA.

Long-tailed Duck

These ground nesting ducks are widely dispersed across the arctic wetlands around the world. They winter in shallow waters near the shores of oceans in unfrozen large freshwater lakes. They feed on aquatic molluscs and crustaceans, which in turn feed by filtering large amounts of water to harvest zoo plankton. Thus the ducks are at the top of a food chain that channels any pollutants into their bodies. PCBs, organochlorine pesticides, polycyclic aromatic hydrocarbons and trace elements are all found in long-tailed ducks and scaup which feed in similar habitats. Fortunately, so far pollutants haven't reached lethal levels for goldeneyes. Waterfowl are important biomonitors of aquatic environments.

Harlequin duck (*Histrionicus histrionicus*). Male standing in rapids. A spectacular, colorfully dressed sea duck. Its name comes from the Latin word "Histiro" meaning "actor." European harlequins breed only in Iceland. Others breed in Greenland, western Canada and Alaska. Harlequin is the only sea duck that can dive in and out of water without pushing off from the water surface. Iceland.

Harlequin Duck

This unique duck spends its summers diving for insect larvae on the bottom of fast flowing mountain streams. They use their webbed feet and wings to fly underwater and use small eddies and upstream currents in rapids to manoeuvre in the fast flowing waters. Even in winter on the ocean shores of North America they dive into the surf to feed before loafing on rocks. They make a very unducklike call which has given them the local name "sea mice." Like all ducks the males play no role in raising the young. They visit the breeding grounds only briefly then return to saltwater coasts for most of the year. Harlequin ducks occur in the northwestern mountains of North America and the eastern mountains of Labrador and Quebec. The eastern population was recently tracked in winter to remote coasts of southern Greenland. The population is in decline and is endangered in Canada.

Arctic terns mating (*Sterna paradisaea*). The tern is well known for its long, yearly migration from the Arctic to Antarctica, a round trip of 80,000 km. Svalbard, Norway.

Arctic Tern

Red-billed and red-legged, the arctic tern is very similar to the common tern except for the black tip on its beak. The arctic tern has a worldwide circumpolar breeding range. They mate for life and return to the colony each year. The oldest birds return first. The nest is a shallow hollow on open tundra or rocky islands and beaches often lined with small rocks or plant material. The arctic tern is well known for its long, yearly migration from pole to pole, from its northern arctic breeding grounds to Antarctica. It is the longest migration route known.

In Antarctica they will spend four to five months before traveling back to the arctic region arriving home in May or June. The arctic tern receives more sunlight per year than any other bird as it spends the summer where there is 24 hours of daylight and enjoys another summer at its wintering grounds in Antarctica. Arctic terns are aggressively defensive of their nests with eggs or young chicks. They will divebomb humans as well as predators such as polar bear, wolf, arctic fox, skua and jaeger, striking the head and back drawing blood from unprotected areas.

Arctic tern. During bonding, the male courts the female with a small capelin. Vallda Sandö, Sweden.

Ross's gull (*Rhodostethia rosea*). This gull was first discovered 1823 in Foxe Basin, Nunavut, Canada. Hudson Bay, Churchill, Canada.

Ross's Gull

This small, dovelike gull is named after the British Arctic explorer James Clark Ross, 1800-1862. Ross's gull was an Arctic mystery bird, first discovered in the Foxe Basin, Nunavut, Canada in 1823. Not until 80 years later was this bird's nesting area found in Siberia's Kolyma River delta. These birds are also found breeding on the Southern Taimyr Peninsula and the Lena River delta. Known sporadic nesting sites are in Greenland, Svalbard and Churchill, Canada. Ross's gulls prefer nesting together with arctic terns on the tundra, river estuaries and small lake islets. It migrates only short distances from its summer nesting areas and spends the winters on northern latitudes close to the pack ice in Bering Sea, Barents Sea and the Sea of Okhotsk. The Ross's gull is one of the most sought after species by birdwatchers in North America, Scandinavia and Europe.

Flock of mature ivory gulls (*Pagophila eburnea*). The gulls are opportunistic scavengers often feeding on seals killed by polar bears. Svalbard, Norway.

Ivory Gull

The ivory gull was described by Constantine Phipps in 1774 from a specimen collected on Svalbard. These gulls inhabit the arctic ice floes and endure a harsh, inhospitable environment. The species has declined rapidly and suddenly pushed the world's only all white gull onto Canada's Endangered Species list. It breeds in colonies throughout the Canadian Arctic, Greenland, Svalbard, Jan Mayen and islands off northern Russia. No records show the ivory gull breeding in Alaska. They nest on rocky islands and cliff ledges near pack ice. The gulls are opportunistic scavengers often found feeding on seals killed by polar bears. The ivory gull migrates only short distances and winters at the edge of the pack ice or near polynyas, open water surrounded by sea ice.

Immature ivory gull showing variable amounts of black on the face and dark spots on the body. Simrishamn, Sweden.

Glaucous Gull

A large gull which breeds in the extreme high Arctic of Alaska, Canada, Greenland, Iceland, Svalbard and eastern Russia. The back and wings of the gull are a light whitish gray and can be confused with the glaucous-winged gull which has darker gray wings and back. However, this gull breeds only on the west coast of Alaska and islands in the Bering Sea. The glaucous gull is a predator and scavenger of seabirds, robbing their nests of eggs and chicks. They also feed on seal carcass leftovers from polar bear kills, a major part of their diet during the winter months. Partially migratory, the gull winters farther north than most gulls, remaining on the breeding grounds throughout the year. Some of these birds remain in open water close to the pack ice of the Barents and Bering Seas.

Glaucous gull (*Larus hyperboreus*). Female and male communicating. This high Arctic bird has the fitting Latin name "hyperboreus" meaning "beyond the north wind." Svalbard, Norway.

Great black-backed gull (*Larus marinus*) voicing opinion. This is the largest gull in the world. Lauvsnes archipelago, Norway.

Common Gull and Mew Gull

The species distribution is circumpolar except for Greenland. The species is split into three subspecies. The ones in Europe and Asia are together known as "common gull." They breed in Fennoscandia north to Barents Sea and east across northern Russia to Kamchatka. The subspecies in North America is called mew gull. It breeds only along the Alaska coast south to British Columbia, Canada. Colonies have bred on Iceland since 1936 on wet tundra, small lake islets, swamps and marshes. Colony size varies from two to 300 pairs. They nest on the ground and in scrubby spruce and pine trees where they construct a shapeless nest of small branches and other plant material. Breeding season begins in late May, usually one to four eggs are laid and hatch after 24–26 days. Like most gulls, they eat all kinds of food and will scavenge as well as hunt for small prey.

Left: Common gull (*Larus canus canus*). Male and female during spring migration on an icebound lake in northern Finland.

Great Black-backed Gull

The great black-backed gull is the largest gull in the world with a wingspan of 140 to 150 cm and weighs up to 2 kg. In the 1800's the gull was harvested for its feathers which were used for fashionable ladies' hats, leading to extinction from large parts of its range. Some populations that were once severely endangered have recovered during the 20th century. Recovery of these gulls has been attributed to the fishery industry in the North and Norwegian Seas. The great black-backed gull breeds along the coasts of Sweden, Norway and Russia's east coast to Novaya Zemlya. The gull is an efficient predator and scavenger eating eggs, chicks and ducklings. It also kills larger birds like common murres and can catch adult dovekie and puffins in flight.

Fireweed (*Chamerion angustifolium*) growing along the lake shore of Torneträsk, 150 km north of the Arctic Circle. The lake, 168 m deep is the second deepest in Sweden, gouged out by ice age glaciers. Lappland, Sweden.

CHAPTER TWELVE

Tundra Beauties and Berries

Tundra Beauties

The beauty of spectacular spring flowers covering the arctic tundra is one of the most marvellous displays of summer. Spring in the high Arctic starts with the sun melting the snowpack and warming the ground surface, triggering plant sprouting. However, some plants will start growing under the melting snow. Flower buds, which developed late during the previous summer are ready to explode in an array of yellow, blue, red and purple after their long winter of dormancy.

Flowers are colorful in order to attract insects carrying pollen from flower to flower. Different colors attract different insects. Blue, red and purple attract bumblebees; yellow and white attract flies. The length of the active growing season varies according to weather, location and elevation. It can be less than a month, restricting plant height and dwarfing some species.

Fireweed along the lake in front of Spencer Glacier, Chugach National Forest, Alaska, USA.

Immature hairy lousewort (*Pedicularis hirsuta*). Svalbard, Norway.

Mature hairy lousewort (*Pedicularis hirsuta*). Svalbard, Norway.

Hairy Lousewort

Hairy lousewort is a perennial green root parasitic plant.
Suckers on the roots attach to other plants absorbing food from
them. Starch is stored in the roots making a valued food source
for the Inuit and bears. The immature hairy lousewort is coated
with white woolly hairs protecting the flower buds from frost
on the harsh arctic tundra. This flower ranges throughout the
polar regions of Greenland, Svalbard, Norway, Russia, Alaska
and Canada.

Dwarf Fireweed

**Dwarf fireweed has circumboreal distribution throughout
the northern hemisphere including the subarctic and arctic.**
Like its sister species the taller fireweed, every part of the dwarf
fireweed is edible and valuable nutrition for the Inuit who eat
the leaves raw as a salad with meals of seal and walrus blubber.
The fleshy leaves when cooked taste much like spinach. This is
the national flower of Greenland.

Right: Dwarf fireweed (*Chamerion latifolium*). On the Canadian tundra it is
known as river beauty willowherb. Greenland.

Mountain harebell (*Campanula lasiocarpa*). This native harebell is a western North American species confined to rocky alpine slopes. Canadian Rockies.

Whitish gentian (*Gentiana algida*). A high altitude species blooming into late September. Denali National Park, Alaska, USA.

Mountain Harebell

A beautiful alpine plant, the mountain harebell has a single deep lilac bluebell-shaped flower up to 3 cm long on a stem of only 1–15 cm. This harebell is a native western North American species in Alaska, Yukon, Northwest Territories, Alberta and British Columbia. It is confined to rocky alpine slopes and ridges high above the timberline.

Whitish Gentian

Whitish gentian grows on stony slopes and alpine meadows up to 1,500 m elevation. The attractive funnel shaped flowers grow up to 5 cm long. They are mostly yellowish-white but sometimes purple blue striped on the outside. It ranges throughout the Northern Hemisphere. A high altitude species blooms into late September.

Nootka Lupine

Nootka lupine is a common native species ranging across Alaska's Aleutian Island chain and Pribilof Islands south along the west coast of North America. In Iceland, the Nootka lupine was imported and planted on the black desert sand to stop erosion. Lupine, especially the seeds, are very poisonous.

Right: Nootka lupine (*Lupinus nootkatensis*), Pribilof Islands, Alaska. In Iceland, the Nootka lupine was imported and planted on the black desert to stop sand erosion.

Purple mountain saxifrage (*Saxifrage oppositifolia*). The world's most northerly flowering species growing within 713.5 km south of the North Pole. Svalbard, Norway.

Western moss heather (*Cassiope mertensiana*). The white bellshaped flower traps heat inside the bell which gives the plant extra energy to produce fruit. Canadian Rockies.

Purple Mountain Saxifrage

Purple mountain saxifrage is common in the high Arctic, across North America and Eurasia. Preferring rocky habitat, it is one of the first spring flowers to bloom along the edge of the melting snowpack. It has been found on Kaffeklubben Island in north Greenland, within 713.5 km of the North Pole, making it the world's most northerly flower species. The Inuit use the stems and leaves to make tea and as a tobacco substitute. This is the territorial flower of Nunavut, Canada.

Western Moss Heather

Native to western North America, western moss heather is found in open subalpine areas from Alaska south to Northern California. Heat trapped inside the white bellshaped flower gives the plant extra energy to produce fruit. Western moss heather can be used to produce a golden brown dye.

Larkspurleaf Monkshood

Larkspurleaf monkshood wolfsbane contains alkaloids that are very poisonous if ingested by humans and animals. Historically, the toxin extracted from the genus Aconitum was used to kill wolves and other predators as well as rodent pests. Even skin contact can cause numbness. The monkshood flower is light blue with an upper sepal shaped like a monk's hood. This northern monkshood is at home in meadows, thickets, stream banks and rocky slopes in the subalpine and alpine zones. It ranges across Alaska and western Canada.

Larkspurleaf monkshood (*Aconitum delphiniifolium*), historically known as wolfbane. The toxin extracted from the Aconitum family was used to kill wolves. Ivvavik National Park, Yukon, Canada.

Moss campion (*Silene acaulis*). Here covered with purple flowers, the bright green moss-like clump is well adapted to withstand harsh weather ranging from hot sunlight to high winds and intense cold. Canadian Rockies.

Moss Campion

Moss campion is a small and mosslike tough groundhugging plant forming densely matted round cushions, each of which grows as a separate island that can spread out to more than 1 m across. Each bright green island absorbs the sun's warming rays, generating a microclimate several degrees above that of the outside air. It can withstand weather extremes including intense sunlight, high winds, and the cold of winter. In Alaska some of these cushion islands have survived for more than 300 years. The plants are common in high mountain regions well above the timberline and on the arctic tundra across Alaska, Greenland and Russia. They also grow on Svalbard as well as on Russia's Wrangel Island.

Svalbard poppy (*Papaver dahlianum*). Poppy flowers are heliotropic meaning they turn towards the sun and follow its movements which can continue around the clock in the land of the midnight sun. Svalbard, Norway.

Svalbard Poppy – Alaska Poppy

Svalbard poppy and Alaska poppy have both yellow and white flowers. Poppies are native worldwide. They are one of the most stunning flowers on the arctic tundra and high mountain ranges where they favor rocky ridges and scree slopes well above timberline. The poppy's delicate flower petals are said to be heliotropic meaning they turn towards the sun and follow its arc across the sky. In the "Land of the midnight sun" they compensate for the short summer by staying open around the clock moving to catch sunlight while they attract pollinating flies and fuzzy bumblebees.

Right: Alaska poppy (*Papaver alaskanum*). Pribilof Islands, Alaska, USA.

Crowberry (*Empetrum nigrum*). Hardy groundhugging evergreen berries are nearly tasteless until frost turns the starch to sugar and they sweeten to the delight of wildlife. Wapusk National Park, Canada.

Crowberry

Crowberry, also called blackberry or mossberry, is a species with circumboreal distribution. This hardy ground hugging evergreen produces watery berries with little taste until the first frost change its carbohydrates to sugar. The berries persist on the plants through winter and can be picked in the spring, making them a good food source year round for First Nations, Inuit and Sami peoples as well as for bears, willow and rock ptarmigans.

Cloudberry (*Rubus chamaemorus*) are called hjortron in Sweden where they are made into jam and used as a topping for pancakes and waffles. Arctic Canada.

Cloudberry

Cloudberry is native to tundra and alpine areas around the world. These low growing perennial plants grow 5–20 cm high. They are unisexual, having male and female flowers produced on separate plants. In Scandinavia cloudberries are common on peat bogs and moist ground. In early August the ripe golden colored fruit is very juicy, delicious and rich in vitamin C. In Sweden cloudberries are called hjortron and are made into jam for toppings on pancakes and waffles. In Finland the tasty Lakka liqueur is made from cloudberries. Cloudberry flowers are frost sensitive but the plant itself can withstand temperatures well below -40°C.

Lingonberry

Lingonberry is native to the boreal forest and arctic tundra across the Northern Hemisphere from North America to Eurasia. The name lingonberry originates from its Swedish name lingon. The species keeps its green leaves year round even in the coldest years, enduring temperatures that can go below -40°C. In Sweden lingonberries are made into jam and juice that are considered part of a staple diet. Norway produces Lillehammer berry liqueur, a centuries old recipe.

Lingonberry (*Vaccinium vitis-idaea*). The name originates from its Swedish name lingon. Yukon, Canada.

In late August and early September bearberry enhances the arctic tundra with its crimson deep veined leaves. Northwest Territories, Canada.

Berries and Berry Eaters

The plants that produce berries spread by having their seeds dispersed and fertilized with dung by berry eaters like ptarmigan and other members of the grouse family. To entice fruit eaters, berries become sugary but only once the seeds are ripe, not before. If seeds are eaten while immature they won't germinate. Ripe berries change color from green to red or black, signalling fruit eaters that the berries are ready to eat. Most berries ripen in autumn creating such a glut of food that some berries remain uneaten, wasted from the plant's perspective. A few plant species keep berries unripe until spring. Cold winter temperatures convert starches to sugars and these species avoid competition by ripening in the spring, much to the benefit of very hungry berry eaters.

Alpine Blueberry

Alpine blueberry (*Vaccinium uliginosum*). This species of blueberry can grow on bedrock containing uranium and still survive. Northwest Territories, Canada.

Alpine blueberry is a low growing shrub also known as northern bilberry or bog blueberry. It is found in alpine and high latitude boreal forests of Europe, Asia and North America. Alpine blueberry can even grow on bedrock uranium. Where this is the only plant that grows on bedrock, it is a good indicator of the metal for geologists. When elemental uranium collects in the leaves and fruit, they can be somewhat dangerous to eat. However, in uranium free soil the berries are edible and sweet, a traditional food source for North America's First Nations, as well as several species of grouse, small wildlife and bears.

Alpine Bearberry

Alpine bearberry has a circumpolar distribution at high latitudes across North America, Greenland, Scandinavia and Russia. Fruit is first green, then red, finally when ripe, shining black. Bearberries form a symbiotic relationship with fungus rhizomes which supply it with nutrients such as phosphorous. Bearberries are a favorite food for bears and tundra birds such as willow and rock ptarmigan. First Nations people use the leaves for tobacco. Beginning in late August or early September, the alpine bearberry leaves explode in a blaze of flaming crimson, covering the tundra in a spectacular blanket of color.

Alpine bearberry ripe fruit (*Arctostaphylos alpina*). Bearberries are a favorite food for bears and tundra birds. Canadian Rockies.

Net-veined willow (*Salix reticulata*). Also known as snow willow, this small dwarf shrub is native to northern Scandinavia, Asia and North America. Canada.

Net-veined Willow

Net-veined willow is a circumpolar small dwarf species native to northern Scandinavia, Asia and North America. It has small 1–2 cm long net-veined leathery leaves. Their waxy coating prevents loss of moisture in the dry arctic climate. It is related to the arctic willow (*Salix arctica*), the world's most northerly woody plant. One specimen 236 years old was found in eastern Greenland. Arctic willow bark and twigs are high in vitamin C with a sweet taste, making them a rich food source for arctic caribou, muskoxen, hares, ground squirrels, lemmings and some birds. During the winter, willow buds are the main food source for rock and willow ptarmigan.

Arctic Bumblebee

Arctic bumblebee has a circumpolar distribution. Its thick fur reduces heat loss and by making its muscles shiver it can heat its body up to +35°C. This and the long summer arctic days enable bumblebees to fly in all kinds of weather and all hours of the day, collecting nectar and pollen from flowers and many species of willow. Bumblebees are common in North America with 46 species north of Mexico. Recently, a northern European bumblebee was collected in Alaska.

Arctic bumblebee (*Bombus polaris*) feeding on felt-leaved willow (*Salix alaxensis*), Brooks Range, Alaska.

Arctic Woolly Bear

Arctic woolly bear moth is found within the Arctic Circle of Greenland and Canada. They feed on arctic willow during June, then spend the rest of summer dormant within a protective cocoon as their body prepares for being frozen during the coming winter. With such a short growing season, this moth can take over seven years to complete its life cycle from egg to adult moth. Because of their thick fur they are unique among moths and butterflies being able to withstand temperatures below -60°C — a unique combination of adaptation to polar extremes.

Arctic woolly bear (*Gynaephora groenlandica*), Kekerten Island, Nunavut, Baffin Island, Canada.

CHAPTER THIRTEEN

Melting Arctic: A Matter of Time

Polar Ice Caps and Glaciers

Freshwater, in the form of glaciers and ice caps, is impacted by global warming. Worldwide, 85% of glaciers are shrinking including those in polar regions. In North America, between 1970 and 2000, mountain glaciers lost up to half their ice and the melting continues. The largest ice shelf in the Arctic is the Ward Hunt Shelf, located on the northern tip of Ellesmere Island in Arctic Canada. In 2003, scientists were astonished when it cracked in half. Climate warming was the reason. The world's two largest ice caps are in Greenland and Antarctica. They contain roughly 70% of our planet's freshwater. Just as rivers drain water from lakes, countless frozen rivers, called glaciers, bleed ice from these ice caps into surrounding oceans. Enormous chunks of ice that break off into the sea are called icebergs. In recent decades the speed of glacial flow has accelerated, discharging more icebergs into the oceans and reducing the overall thickness of the ice caps. Between 2002 and 2009, annual ice loss from both polar ice caps doubled, accelerating from 137 to 286 billion tons in Greenland and from 104 to 246 billion tons in Antarctica.

Why is ice draining off these ice caps at an accelerating rate? When meltwater on the surface of a glacier drains through cracks in the ice down to bedrock, it theoretically lubricates the surface of the bedrock, allowing glacial ice to slide over it more quickly.

Left: Freshwater running from Nordaustlandet ice cap on Svalbard, one of the largest storehouses of arctic ice outside Greenland. Nearly 60% of Svalbard is glaciated and the island is losing ice mass at an accelerating rate. Norway.

A large slab of ice calving from an advancing Alaska tidewater glacier. USA.

Global warming impacts the marine ecosystem. Glacial ice that flows into the oceans eventually melts. So much ice is now melting that sea levels have risen 10 to 20 cm in the last 100 years. Half of this is from the melting ice caps and half is from the expansion of the sea water as it has warmed. Researchers predict that if 50% of both the Greenland ice cap and the Antarctic ice cap melted, global sea levels would rise 5.5–6 m, potentially displacing 180 million people currently living in coastal areas. Arctic warming has not only elevated sea levels but reduced the area and thickness of sea ice.

Since 1980 pack ice coverage has declined by 5.5% during winters and 18% during summers. Ice thinning was first documented by an unexpected source. In the 1950's, British, American and Russian submarines began to patrol the Arctic Ocean because it was the shortest route between North America and Europe. The patrols kept records of the ice thickness because they needed to know where it would be thin enough to break through for the sub to surface. When the military was finally persuaded to share their data with ice scientists, they discovered that since 1980 the sea ice had thinned by roughly half.

Greenland Ice sheet in 1987. The second largest ice sheet in the world after Antarctica. Mountain peaks sticking up through an ice sheet are called nunataks. During the ice age they were refuges for animal and plant species that otherwise would have been destroyed by the ice.

Since the 1990's there has been a marked change in arctic weather patterns. Prevailing winds and currents in the Beaufort Sea have shifted eastward towards Fram Strait, the passage between Greenland and Svalbard. The strait is the major outlet for the Arctic Ocean. Thus the reduction in summer sea ice may be a combination of enhanced flushing through Fram Strait, as well as increased melting and thinning. Many researchers predict that by 2050, the Arctic may be ice free during summer. Others suggest it could happen even sooner, perhaps as early as 2030. White sea ice reflects the sun's heat back into the sky. As the sea ice disappears, that solar energy is instead absorbed by the sea, raising its temperature even higher. Less pack ice also means there is more open water to generate the clouds that grow storms, as well as less barrier to dampen ocean swells. Both those changes increase storm surges pounding the coastlines, especially at high tide. In Alaska alone, 60 coastal communities are at risk of being washed away. In recent years, the Yukon-Kuskokwim and Mackenzie River Deltas have been inundated with sea water up to 35 km inland. The wetlands of both deltas are important waterfowl nesting areas. Coastal flooding also accelerates the thawing of permafrost and increases erosion. On average, Alaska loses more than 1 m of coastline every year.

Snout of Turnstone Glacier 1994. Located in Quttinirpaaq National Park at latitude 81 degrees north in the NE corner of Ellesmere Island, Nunavut. This park is the second largest in Canada after Wood Buffalo National Park. It is also the second most northerly park on Earth, after Northeast Greenland National Park.

A piedmont glacier 1999, flowing from Henrietta-Nesmith Glacier in Quttinirpaaq National Park — in Inuktitut language "quittinirpaaq" means "top of the world." Ellesmere Island, Nunavut. Canada.

Threatened Wildlife

Global warming impacts every level of the arctic food chain from invertebrates at the bottom, progressing through fish, birds and mammals. The invertebrates are the spineless wonders of the natural world, overlooked by many but vital to the health and integrity of the Arctic. The smallest among them are plankton, tiny organisms drifting in the sea. Warm water favors smaller forms of plankton which are eaten by juvenile fish and smaller seabirds. As arctic seas have heated up, the mix of plankton species has changed, altering fish and seabird populations. Among the seabirds, the most heavily impacted have been the smaller members of the auk family, namely dovekies, least and crested auklets.

Another possible impact from the melting sea ice may be increased predation on bottom-dwelling invertebrates like marine worms, snails, clams, crabs, and starfish. As the protective mantle of ice disappears, these invertebrates become vulnerable to deep-diving sea ducks such as eiders and scoters. Arctic invertebrates are also threatened by ocean acidification. Roughly a quarter of the carbon dioxide we humans dump into the atmosphere dissolves in the oceans forming carbonic acid. The acidity erodes corals and shells of snails, clams and mussels which are composed of calcium carbonate. This erosion can be fatal.

Warmer seas warm the body of fish increasing their metabolic rate and food needs which is especially stressful for juvenile fish. Furthermore, the warmer seas have led to the invasion of the southern arctic by temperate fish species that were not present in the past. Changing fish populations force diet changes for predators such as seabirds, seals and whales. For example, in the Atlantic, capelin now range farther north than in the past. In Hudson Bay, capelin have replaced arctic cod as the most abundant fish in their size range but capelin have less body fat than arctic cod. The question becomes, can seabirds and marine mammals adjust to a new prey species?

Piedmont glacier in Quttinirpaaq National Park 1995. Glaciers are formed at the foot of mountains by discharge of ice from one or more confined valley glaciers. Ellesmere Island, Nunavut, Canada.

Adult ivory gull (*Pagophila eburnea*). The Latin name means "ivory colored sea ice lover." Svalbard Archipelago, Norway.

Birds, a conspicuous element of the Arctic, are also impacted by climate change. Examples are the decline of numerous shorebirds, partially in response to disappearing tundra nesting habitats, the wetlands succumb to melting permafrost and the imposed stress of dietary shifts among plankton-feeding auks. The warming Arctic has also led to reduction in the climate barrier to disease. Pathogens are now appearing where they were never seen before. In recent years, avian cholera has killed thousands of arctic nesting birds like common eiders and snow geese.

One bird species, the ivory gull, deserves special mention because of its dramatic population decline — 80% since 1980 in Canada. This is due to melting pack ice and possibly to mercury poisoning. The ivory gull's scientific name (*Pagophila eburnea*), means "the ivory colored sea ice lover." The name is appropriate as the ivory gull is more reliant on the pack ice than any other arctic bird. On the ice, it scavenges marine mammal carcasses often from polar bear kills. The bird also hunts for arctic cod and amphipods associated with the shifting ice.

Arctic fox (*Alopex lagopus*) in transitional summer pelage. The arctic fox has increasing competition from the red fox which has moved north because of global warming. Since 1918 the red fox has advanced to 1,000 km north of the Arctic Circle, 1,500 km from the nearest forest. Victoria Island, Nunavut, Canada.

The arctic fox is another northern mammal impacted by climate change due less to increasing temperatures than to increasing competition. The competition comes from the red fox, one of the most successful carnivores on the planet. Previously, the arctic fox and the red fox occupied different habitats; the arctic fox kept to the tundra and the red fox stayed in the forests south of the tree line. In North America, the situation began to change in the early 1900's as red foxes moved north. By 1918, the russet carnivores had crossed over from the Ungava Peninsula to southern Baffin Island. Within 45 years they had reached the southern end of Ellesmere Island, 1,000 km north of the Arctic Circle and 1,500 km from the nearest forest.

The red fox, which is 60% heavier and 25% larger than the arctic fox is physically superior. It dominates any combat, sometimes even killing arctic fox. The arctic fox, however, is thermally superior to its larger rival. Its smaller ears and muzzle, shorter legs and thicker pelt translate into greater retention of body heat. It can withstand much colder temperatures. The arctic fox's critical minimum temperature is -45°C versus -13°C for the red fox. Finally, because the arctic fox weighs less than its russet relative, it needs less food to maintain itself and can better survive the unpredictability of prey supply. Competition and the climate warming have pushed the arctic fox ever farther north in North America and on the tundra of northern Russia. Global warming is forcing a new spatial equilibrium for many species.

Barren-ground caribou bulls on the arctic tundra (*Rangifer tarandus groenlandicus*). Climate change will endanger circumpolar habitats for caribou and reindeer. Researchers estimate the distinct Canadian caribou lineage could shrink 90% by 2070. Yukon, Canada.

Impacts on the Megafauna

Impacts on the charismatic megafauna of the Arctic, the big hairy mammals, have grabbed media interest in stories about global warming. Among the hoofed mammals, muskoxen and caribou have seen the greatest changes. In a normal winter, both muskox and caribou forage for grasses and sedges by pawing through the snow with their sharp edged front hooves. In recent decades, warmer winters have led to mid winter thaws. When the temperatures dip, which they invariably do, the tundra becomes encased in impenetrable ice. The animals starve if they cannot locate better feeding areas. In 1997, for example, 90% of the Peary caribou in high Arctic Canada died from mid winter ground icing. In 2014, icing starved 14,000 reindeer in Russia's Yamal region. Worldwide, there has been a 60% decline in caribou populations resulting from a combination of global warming and overhunting. Global warming has two other important repercussions on caribou. The recent northward advance of shrub tundra reduces the amount of habitat where caribou can successfully forage. Longer, warmer summers also increase the harassment by bloodsucking insects which hamper a caribou's ability to forage and gain weight.

Bull Peary caribou (*Rangifer tarandus pearyi*). The caribou is white in winter and slate gray in summer with white on legs and underparts. In 1997, mid winter ground icing killed 90% of the Peary caribou in Canada's high Arctic. Banks Island, Northwest Territories, Canada.

Up until 10,000 years ago, the Beringia steppe-tundra was an enormous ice free ecological refugium that supported large mammals like woolly mammoth, giant bison, muskoxen and Przewalski's horse. Beringia Winter Scene, Government of Yukon/Artist George "Rinaldino" Teichman, 1997.

Woolly mammoth (*Mammuthus primigenius*). Scientists have estimated the woolly mammoth disappeared from the Northern Hemisphere mainland near the end of the last ice age, 10,000 to 14,000 years ago as the glaciers melted and sea levels rose. The populations survived 6,000 years ago on Alaska's Saint Paul Island in the Pribilofs and 4,000 years ago on Russia's Wrangel Island in the Chukchi Sea. Island mammoths tended to be dwarfs, allowing for larger populations, greater genetic diversity, and higher survival chances than would have been possible with an equal distribution of larger mammoths. Display at Royal British Columbia Museum, Victoria, B.C., Canada.

Muskoxen bulls (*Ovibos moschatus*). Taimyr Peninsula was apparently the last refuge for muskoxen in eastern Russia after they disappeared from the rest of that region at least 11,000 years ago. Later they died out on Wrangel Island. However, in 1975, 20 muskoxen were reintroduced to Wrangel Island where the population has since grown to about 200. Wrangel Island, Russia.

The British-Richardson Mountains are an unglaciated mountain range. Only a little of this ecoregion was covered by glaciers or ice sheets during the last Pleistocene ice age which ended about 11,500 years ago. Warmer summers with longer growing periods allowed the scrub forest of herbs, shrubs and trees like white spruce, dwarf birch and willow to spread farther north onto the alpine tundra. Ivvavik National Park, Yukon, Canada.

Pacific walrus (*Odobenus rosmarus divergens*). Herd resting on a melting ice floe during spring breakup. Climate warming has sharply reduced the thickness and extent of arctic sea ice forcing walruses to haul out on land to rest where they are more vulnerable to polar bears. Chukchi Sea, Alaska, USA.

Today, walruses are located only in the Arctic. However, this wasn't always so; 350 years ago there were perhaps 500,000 walruses in the Magdalen Islands in the Gulf of St. Lawrence and another 100,000 on Sable Island off the eastern shore of Nova Scotia. Walruses ranged as far south as Cape Cod, Massachusetts. They later disappeared because of overhunting. Walruses don't need year-round sea ice to thrive. They live in the Arctic today because it's a safe, remote refuge for them. In a warming arctic, walruses may benefit from the loss of sea ice, giving them access to bottom feeding areas that were previously protected by continuous ice cover. The thinning and melting of the sea ice may help them greatly as long as they are safe from polar bears when they haul out on land to rest.

More has been written about global warming and the impact it's having on the polar bear than the effect on any other arctic creature. The polar bear (*Ursus maritimus*), is a marine bear and reliant on sea ice for hunting, travel, courting and mating. As arctic sea ice thins and melts, polar bears are dangerously affected. The most critical hunting period for a polar bear is from March to July when newly weaned seal pups are abundant, padded with 50% fat, and naive about predators. During these critical months a bear will consume and store roughly 70% of its total annual energy needs. The disappearing sea ice results in a shorter hunting season and smaller fat reserves for polar bears. This, in turn, leads to declining survival and reproduction rates.

The polar bears of western Hudson Bay have been studied since the 1960's, longer than any other polar bear population. They are also the most southern population of polar bears and the most vulnerable to global warming. Among all bear populations, pregnant females need the largest fat reserves. In 1980, the average pregnant female in western Hudson Bay weighed 290 kg. By 2004, the average weight had dropped to 230 kg. No female weighing less than 190 kg has ever been recorded with cubs in the spring.

What does the future hold for this magnificent predator? Worldwide, there are 19 subpopulations of polar bear. The Polar Bear Specialist Group, of the International Union for Conservation of Nature has classified population trends as either increasing, stable, declining or unknown. The trends for most of the Russian and Norwegian subpopulations are unknown. The Alaskan sub-populations are declining as are the largest Canadian subpopulations. For the polar bear and most other arctic wildlife species, the future doesn't look promising. Planet Earth needs our attention and help.

Adult polar bear hunting seals on melting pack ice. Svalbard, Norway.

Compared to typical polar bears, this animal's more bulky body, slightly grayish fur, shorter neck, and odd face, suggests it's a grizzly-polar bear hybrid, often referred to as a "grolar" bear. Arctic Alaska, USA.

Another species that has recently moved northward is the barren ground grizzly bear (*Ursus arctos*). In the 1970's, arctic grizzlies lived throughout Alaska, the Yukon, and the central and western areas of mainland Northwest Territories. In the last four decades the bears have expanded their range, moving eastward towards Hudson Bay and northward into the Western Arctic Banks, Victoria and Melville Islands. Biologists aren't sure if this is the result of global warming or simply the natural outcome of an increasing bear population. The situation has created interesting interactions with their close relative the polar bear. The consequences of this have been unexpected.

In 1991 a male grizzly was seen on the sea ice of Viscount Melville Sound hunting seals. Earlier it had killed a two-year-old polar bear. In 2006, and then again in 2010, hunters killed "hybrid" bears. In both cases the father was a grizzly bear and the mother was either a polar bear or another hybrid. The popular press quickly coined names for the hybrids calling them "grolar" bears or "pizzly" bears. Often, the hybrids are grayish or brownish white, lighter than grizzlies but darker than polar bears. They have a prominent shoulder hump like a grizzly, a neck length between that of a grizzly and a polar bear, and intermediate claws, not as long as a grizzly, but not as curved as a polar bear. No one can predict how global warming will affect the balance between the two species.

Polar bears (*Ursus maritimus*) occasionally kill and eat one another, especially when their normal marine mammal prey is scarce. Berries, bird eggs and seaweed will not be enough to support polar bears forced to forage on land as their sea ice hunting season grows ever shorter. Hudson Bay, Canada.

Grizzly (*Ursus arctos*) tend to be smaller than grolar bears and much smaller than polar bears, enabling barren ground grizzlies to obtain enough food on land where larger bears cannot. Banff National Park, Canada.

Sparkling ice wedge pushing up a thawed layer of permafrosted sedge grass soil. Thawing permafrost releases carbon dioxide and methane into the atmosphere. Tibetan Plateau, Ladakh, India.

Permafrost

When permafrost thaws, methane gas is released. Permafrost currently underlies 16–20 million sq. km. of land in the Arctic and Antarctic, totalling an area roughly twice the size of Canada. As the climate is warming, permafrost begins to thaw, releasing methane. The warm waterlogged soil provides ideal conditions for methane production, most of which is slowly, but surely released into the atmosphere.

More than 95% of climate scientists accept the planet is warming and they universally agree that humans are a major cause. Warmer temperatures on the tundra mean the snow melts sooner. This advances the spring thaw and as a result, plants and animals enjoy a longer growing period. Since the 1960's, the growing period in the Arctic has lengthened by 2.5 days per decade. That doesn't sound like much until you consider that for some tundra plants their growing period may only be a few weeks long, every extra day helps. The warmer summer conditions have allowed dwarf willows and birches, cranberries, blueberries and heathers, plants that are characteristic of the southern edge of the tundra, to move farther north.

The warmer conditions have also prompted the arctic tree line to move northwards. East of Hudson Bay, the treeline in northern Quebec has moved 12 km since the 1950's. It is predicted that by 2060 spruce forests will replace two thirds of Alaska's tundra. As the treeline marches north, wildlife move with it. White-tailed deer and moose now range almost as far north as coyotes and red fox.

Waves undercut tundra bluffs on the coastline of the Beaufort Sea exposing permafrost that will be melted by wave action and the sun. Barter Island near the Inupiat village of Kaktovik, Alaska.

Tundra bluff collapsing into the Beaufort Sea exposing permafrost and thin layers of active soil. Barter Island, near the Inupiat village of Kaktovik, Alaska.

Ibyuk Pingo in the Mackenzie River Delta near Tuktoyaktuk. In the arctic and subarctic, if an underground pool of water freezes in winter, the new ice expands in the only direction it can, upwards, forming a hill that is covered with permafrost under an insulating layer of vegetation. Where this happens, century after century, these ice hills called pingos can grow up to 70 m high and 600 m in diameter. Some are conical, others are serpentine, the result of following the course of an old lake or riverbed. Northwest Territories, Canada.

Scientists predict if carbon dioxide levels double, the worldwide arctic tundra will shrink by 40–57%. Loss of tundra breeding habitat will certainly impact arctic-breeding shorebirds. In North America, shorebird populations have already shrunk by 70% since 1973. Three of the shorebird species showing marked declines are the American golden plover, black-bellied plover and Hudsonian godwit. The impact of the loss of tundra on nesting birds may be compounded by habitat changes in their migratory resting areas or on southern wintering grounds.

Freshwater arctic ecosystems are also impacted by rises in air and water temperatures. This has led to longer ice free periods with resulting increased evaporation and shrinkage of many northern lakes. As well, lakes and wetlands resting on permafrost can drain and disappear into subsurface zones when the permafrost thaws. When researchers analyzed satellite images of Russian Siberia from 1973 to 2004, they calculated roughly 11% of 10,000 lakes had disappeared or shrunk drastically because of permafrost thawing; that trend continues today. Tundra lakes are vital habitats for nesting ducks, geese, swans and loons. Habitat loss is one of the biggest challenges faced by wildlife on our planet.

Polygonal patterning in sedge grass tundra is formed in permafrost areas by freezing and thawing of surface water. The geometric forms and patterns are often mistaken for human creations. Ivvavik National Park, Yukon, Canada.

About the Authors

Valerius Geist

1938–2021

Dr. Valerius Geist's career as a zoologist took him to many wild places and allowed him to meet many of the world's great naturalists. He spent nearly two years in northern Canada studying mountain sheep and mountain goats, living isolated in a small cabin and not seeing another human for months on end.

Valerius Geist

Geist focused on how animals communicate, the nature of aggression and status displays, and his mountain sheep work is well known. His interest in the evolution of ice age mammals and humans extended when he became the first Program Director of Environmental Science in the Faculty of Environmental Design, University of Calgary. There he focused on generating environments that maximize human health, and also developed a biological theory on health. He continued to be interested in wild creatures, but turned from academic to applied science and to wildlife conservation.

After 27 years as professor, Valerius retired to pursue his other interests. He is the author of *Deer of the World*, *Buffalo Nation*, *Mule Deer Country*, *Elk Country*, *Wild Sheep Country*, *Antelope Country* and *Mountain Sheep*, for which he won the 1972 Book of the Year Award from The Wildlife Society. Geist was a consultant to the National Geographic Society on several books and television specials.

Geoffrey Holroyd

Dr. Geoffrey Holroyd first visited the Arctic in 1967, when he studied the ecology of breeding songbirds and arctic terns. He earned his PhD from the University of Toronto for his studies of the diet of swallows. He retired after 36 years with the Canadian Wildlife Service, where he headed several arctic research projects.

Geoffrey Holroyd

Holroyd chaired the Peregrine Falcon Recovery Team from 1987-2012 and the Burrowing Owl Recovery Team for eight years. He was adjunct professor in the Department of Renewable Resources at the University of Alberta. He has studied wildlife in many parts of Canada and overseas, including bats in South Africa, blue swallows in Malawi, burrowing owls in the U.S.A. and Mexico, songbirds in Guatemala and owls in Ecuador and Spain.

Holroyd has published over 130 scientific and technical publications and books. He was chair of the Prairie Conservation Action Plan subcommittee of World Wildlife Fund Canada. He organized WWF's first Prairie Conservation and Endangered Species Workshop and served on the organizing committee for most of the subsequent conferences. He also co-edited the proceedings of the first three, and the 10th, Prairie Conservation conferences. He is currently chair of the Beaverhill Bird Observatory, which he co-founded in 1984.

Wayne Lynch

In 1979, when he was 31, Dr. Wayne Lynch left a career in emergency medicine to work full-time as a science writer and photographer. Today, he is Canada's best known and most widely published professional wildlife photographer, as well as a highly acclaimed natural history writer.

Wayne Lynch in the Chilean Andes. Torres del Paine National Park. www.waynelynch.ca

His photo credits include hundreds of magazine covers, thousands of calendar shots, and tens of thousands of images published in over 70 countries. He has contributed photographs and/or text to over 60 natural history books, including: *The Great Northern Kingdom – Life in the Boreal Forest*, *Penguins of the World*, *Bears – Monarchs of the Northern Wilderness*, *Windswept – A Passionate View of the Prairie Grasslands*, *Owls of the United States and Canada – A Complete Guide to their Biology and Behavior*, *A is for Arctic – Natural Wonders of a Polar World*, and *Planet Arctic – Life at the Top of the World*. His books have been described as "a magical combination of words and images."

Dr. Lynch is a Fellow of the internationally recognized Explorers Club, an honour bestowed on those who have actively participated in exploration or have substantially enlarged the scope of human knowledge through scientific achievements and published reports, books and articles. In 1997, he was elected as Fellow of the Arctic Institute of North America, in recognition of his contributions to the knowledge of polar and sub-polar regions. His biography has been included in the Canadian Who's Who since 1996.

Robert Berdan

Dr. Robert Berdan's photographs have won international awards and his photographs have been published in books and magazines – *National Geographic*, *Canadian Geographic*, *Outdoor Photography Canada*, *Photo Life* and others. Berdan received a Doctorate in Cell Biology at Baylor College of Medicine in Houston, Texas.

Robert Berdan www.canadiannaturephotographer.com

He was a researcher and teacher for the University of Alberta and then worked as manager of Education at the Calgary Science Center. He has taught biology, web design, photography and Photoshop. He has published several e-books – *The Art of Canadian Nature Photography*, *Photographing the Aurora*, *Guide to Composition*, *Guide to Your DSLR*, *Best Places to Photograph in Banff and Kananaskis*, and *Macrophotography*.

Index of Vernacular and Scientific Names

Boldface indicates a photograph or illustration. A total of 236 species are listed 21 of them extinct.

Further Reading

Arno, Stephen & Ramona Hammerly. *Timberline – Mountain and Arctic Frontiers*. Seattle: The Mountaineers, 1984.

Bastedo, Jamie. *Falling for Snow – A Naturalist's Journey into the World of Winter*. Calgary: Red Deer Press, 2003.

Brody, Hugh. *Seasons of the Arctic*. San Francisco: A Sierra Club Book, 2000.

Burt, Page. *Barrenland Beauties. Showy Plants of the Arctic Coast*. Yellowknife: Outcrop Ltd., 1991.

Calef, George. *Caribou and the Barren Lands*. Toronto: Firefly Books Ltd., 1981.

Chitty, Dennis. *Do Lemmings Commit Suicide*. Oxford: Oxford University Press, 1996.

Derocher, Andrew. *Polar Bears – A Complete Guide to their Biology and Behavior*. Baltimore: Johns Hopkins University Press, 2012.

Elander, Magnus & Staffan Widstrand. *Vindar Från Arktis*. Stockholm: Prisma, 2008.

Ellis, Richard. *On Thin Ice – The Changing World of the Polar Bear*. New York: Alfred A. Knopf, 2009.

Fagan. Brian. *The Complete Ice Age – How Climate Change Shaped the World*. London: Thames & Hudson, 2009.

Flygare, Hälle. *Storvilt i Canada*. Stockholm: Bonniers, 1970.

Flygare, Hälle. *Buffelmarker*. Kungsbacka: Förlags AB Västra Sverige, 1975.

Fuller, William & John Holmes. *The Life of The Far North*. New York: McGraw-Hill, 1972.

Gaston, Anthony & Ian Jones. *The Auks*. New York: Oxford University Press, 1998.

Geist, Valerius. *Deer of the World – Their Evolution, Behavior and Ecology*. Mechanicsburg: Stackpole Books, 1998.

Geist, Valerius. *Wild Sheep Country*. Minocqua: North Word Press, 1993.

Geist, Valerius. *Buffalo Nation – History and Legend of the North American Bison*. Calgary: Fifth House, 1996.

Geist, Valerius. *Moose – Behaviour, Ecology & Conservation*. Stillwater: Voyageur Press, 1999.

Gellhorn, Joyce. *White-tailed Ptarmigan – Ghosts of the Alpine Tundra*. Boulder: Johnson Books, 2007.

Gray, David. *The Muskoxen of Polar Bear Pass*. Markham: Fitzhenry & Whiteside, 1987.

Halfpenny, James & Roy Douglas Ozanne. *Winter an Ecological Handbook*. Boulder: Johnson Publishing, 1989.

Hambrey, Michael & Jurg Alean. *Glaciers*. Cambridge: Cambridge University Press, 1992.

Hamilton, Garry. *Arctic Fox – Life at the Top of the World*. Richmond Hill: Firefly Books Ltd., 2008.

Heinrich, Bernard. *Winter World – The Ingenuity of Animal Survival*. New York: Harper Collins Publishers, 2003.

Henry, David. *Canada's Boreal Forest*. Washington: Smithsonian Press, 2002.

Kazlowski, Steven. *The Last Polar Bear*. Seattle: Braided River, 2008.

Kurten, Björn. *The Age of Mammals*. New York: Columbia University Press, 1972.

Kurten, Björn. *Istidens djurvärld*. Stockholm: Bonniers, 1964.

Lange, Ian. *Ice Age Mammals of North America – A Guide to the Big, the Hairy, and the Bizarre*. Missoula: Mountain Press, 2002.

Lynch, Wayne. *A is for Arctic – Natural Wonders of a Polar World*. Willowdale: Firefly Books Ltd., 1996.

Lynch, Wayne. *Planet Arctic – Life at the Top of the World.* Richmond Hill: Firefly Books Ltd., 2010.

Lynch, Wayne. *Owls of the United States and Canada.* Baltimore: Johns Hopkins University Press, 2007.

Lynch, Wayne. *The Great Northern Kingdom – Life in the Boreal Forest.* Markham: Fitzhenry and Whiteside, 2001.

Martin, Paul. *Twilight of the Mammoths – Ice Age Extinctions and the Rewilding of America.* Berkeley: University of California Press, 2005.

Mehlum, Fridtjof. *Birds and Mammals of Svalbard.* Oslo: Norsk Polarinstitut, 1990.

Meurs, Rinie van. *Polar Odyssey.* Haarlem: Ger Meesters Boekproducties, 2000.

Ogilvie, M.A. *The Winter Birds – Birds of the Arctic.* New York: Praeger Publishers, 1976.

Paine, Stefani. *The Nature of Arctic Whales.* Vancouver: Greystone Books, 1995.

Pedersen, Alwin. *Polar Animals.* New York: Taplinger Publishing, 1966.

Perry, Richard. *The Polar Worlds.* New York: Taplinger Publishing, 1973.

Peterson, Randolph. *North American Moose.* Toronto: University of Toronto Press, 1955.

Pielou, E.C. *After the Ice Age – The Return of Life to Glaciated North America.* Chicago: University of Chicago Press, 1991.

Pielou, E.C. *A Naturalist's Guide to the Arctic.* Chicago: University of Chicago Press, 1994.

Rendahl H. & Alwin Pedersen. *Arktiska Fåglar.* Stockholm: Åhlen & Söners Förlag, 1936.

Riedman, Marianne. *The Pinnipeds: Seals, Sea Lions, and Walruses.* Berkeley: University of California Press, 1990.

Rosing, Norbert. *The World of the Polar Bear.* Richmond Hill: Firefly Books Ltd., 2006.

Russell, John. *The World of the Caribou.* San Francisco: A Sierra Club Book, 1998.

Sale, Richard. *A Complete Guide to Arctic Wildlife.* Richmond Hill: Firefly Books Ltd., 2006.

Scotter, George & Hälle Flygare. *Wildflowers of the Rocky Mountains.* North Vancouver: Whitecap Books, 2007.

Sneed, Collard. *Hopping Ahead of Climate Change.* Missoula: Mountain Press Publishing, 2016.

Sterling, Ian. *Polar Bears.* Ann Arbor: University of Michigan Press, 1988.

Stonehouse, Bernard. *Animals of the Arctic – The Ecology of the Far North.* New York: Holt, Rinehart & Winston, 1971.

Thomas, David. *Frozen Oceans – The Floating World of Pack Ice.* London: Natural History Museum, 2004.

Thompson, Ernest. *The Arctic Prairies.* New York: Harper and Row Publishers, 1981.

Torkildsen, Torbjørn – Editor. *Svalbard – Vårt Nordligaste Norge.* Oslo: Det Norske Svalbardselskap, 1984.

Turner, Alan. *Prehistoric Mammals.* Washington: National Geographic, 2004.

Photo Credits

Chapter 1 — Ice Age Survivors

Hälle Flygare: Pages 10, 13, 14 (lower left), 16, 20, 23, 28, 29, 31

Shanttil & Rozinski: Page: 11 (Minden)

Ron Niebrugge: Page 12 (Accent Alaska)

Robin Brandt: Page 14 (upper left) (Accent Alaska)

Donna Dewhurst: Page 18 (Accent Alaska)

Paul Souders: Page 22 (Accent Alaska)

Dorothy Keeler: Page 24 (Accent Alaska)

Donald M. Jones: Page 25 (Minden)

Patrick J. Endres: Page 26

Juan Carlos Munoz: Page 27 (upper left) (Minden)

Wayne Lynch: Page 27 (upper right)

Jim Brandenburg: Page 30 (Minden)

Chapter 2 — Marine Mammals

Hälle Flygare: Pages 32, 33, 37, 39

Sergey Gorshkov: Page 34 (Minden)

Rinie van Meurs: Page 35

Hiroya Minakuchi: Page 36 (Minden)

Masahiro Iijima: Page 38 (Minden)

Hugh Rose: Page 40 (Accent Alaska)

Michael Quinton: Page 41 (Minden)

Sylvain Cordier: Pages 42, 43, 44, 45, 46 (all)

Rolf Hicker: Page 47 (Accent Alaska)

Flip Nicklin: Pages 48 (upper), 49 (all) (Minden)

Kevin Schafer: Page 48 (lower left) (Accent Alaska)

Chapter 3 — Lords of the Arctic

Hälle Flygare: Pages 50 to 56, 58, 59, 61, 62, 63, 65, 67

Rinie van Meurs: Pages 60, 64

Robert Berdan: Page 66

Chapter 4 — Bears of the Northern Hemisphere

Hälle Flygare: Pages 68, 70, 71, 72, 73, 74, 76, 77

Mark Raycroft: Page 69 (Minden)

Jon Cornforth: Page: 75 (Accent Alaska)

Mitsuaki Iwago: Page 78 (Minden)

Jan Vermeer: Page 79 (Minden)

Chapter 5 — Hunters of the Arctic Tundra

Hälle Flygare: Pages 80, 81, 82, 83, 85, 87, 91

Willi Rolfes: Page 84 (Minden)

Sergey Gorshkov: Pages 86, 88 (Minden)

Jasper Doest: Page 89 (upper right) (Minden)

Yva Momatiuk & John Eastcott: Page 89 (lower left) (Minden)

Igor Shpilenok: Page 90 (upper left) (Minden)

Konrad Wothe: Page 90 (lower left) (Minden)

Chapter 6 — Arctic Grazers

Robert Berdan: Page 92

Robin Brandt: Page 93 (Accent Alaska)

Hälle Flygare: Pages 94, 96, 102, 103, 104, 105

Kim Heacox: Page 95 (Accent Alaska)

Rinie van Meurs: Page 97

Mark Raycroft: Page 98 (Minden)

Donna Dewhurst: Page 99 (Accent Alaska)

Doug Herr: Page 100

Michael Quinton: Page 101 (Minden)

Matthias Breiter: Page 106 (Minden)

Jim Brandenburg: Page 107 (upper) (Minden)

Chris Schenk: Page 107 (lower) (Minden)

Donna Dewhurst: Page 108 (Accent Alaska)

Jack Chapman: Page 109 (Minden)

Donald M. Jones: Page 110 (upper) (Minden)

Lasse Olsson: Page 110 (lower)

Klein & M.L. Hubert: Page 111 (Minden)

Chapter 7 — Grouse of Taiga and Tundra

Hälle Flygare: Pages 112, 116, 118, 119, 121, 122, 124, 125

Filippo Nucifora: Page 113 (Minden)

Robert Berdan: Pages 114, 115

Harry Taavetti: Page 117 (upper) (Minden)

Michael Quinton: Page 117 (lower) (Minden)

Göran Engström: Page 120

Sylvain Cordier: Page 123 (upper and lower)